Legal Disclaimer

Liability Disclaimer: Heavenlyz takes steps to ensure that the content of all its publi[illegible] correct. However, errors do occur. Heavenlyz reserves the right to corre[illegible] liability resulting therefrom.

It is not possible for this document to be exhaustive, it is intended to [illegible] level of the[illegible] understanding which self-studying students will then use as a platform to research further material. Most awarding bodies provide documents associated with the qualification being undertaken that are specific and exhaustive for that qualification – students are recommended to obtain these documents (if not already provided) and study their content.

Limitation of Liability: In no event shall Heavenlyz or anyone else involved in the creation, production, or delivery of this publication be liable for any damages whatsoever (including, without limitation, consequential damages including loss of business profits, business interruption, or loss of business information) arising out of the use of, the results of use of this publication, even if Heavenlyz has been advised of the possibility of such damages.

This document and all parts thereof are copyright to Heavenlyz Consultancy. No copying, use or reproduction in any way, in whole or in part, is allowed without prior written permission from Heavenlyz Consultancy Ltd.

Copying, plagiarism or reproduction of any sort without holding a current Heavenlyz Consultancy Ltd approval may lead to prosecution and claims for compensation including but not limited to a proportion of any fee paid by any non-Heavenlyz party in delivery of any product or service, applied currently or retrospectively.

Tel: 01283 703043 Email: liza@heavenlyz.com

CONTENTS

Tel: 01283 703043 Email: liza@heavenlyz.com

1 Authors Welcome

Hello and welcome to the Heavenlyz theory manual. This manual has supported many Animal Care and grooming businesses, charitable establishments, vocations and students.

My name is Liza Cox and I am the lead quality assurance co-ordinator and education manager for Heavenlyz Consultancy Ltd, a business and training consultancy specialising in many fields, including Animal Care and Pet Grooming.

You're in good hands. Heavenlyz is the largest distributed animal care training centre and we operate throughout the UK and Europe. I have worked in the field of animal welfare since 1988 and since 2002 Heavenlyz has provided various services to several awarding organisations and their Accredited Centres. This includes time spent teaching, mentoring and assessing thousands of employers, employees, students and apprentices as well as providing verifier, examiner and moderator services. Heavenlyz has experience not only of delivering qualifications to students, but also in writing those qualifications.

Heavenlyz consultancy can provide many services to both new and existing animal care businesses and has extensive experience of a range of awarding organisation qualifications, including those referenced elsewhere in this book – if, as you read through this manual, you wish to know more about the services that Heavenlyz could offer you then please contact us on 01283 703043 or liza@heavenlyz.com.

Heavenlyz Consultancy Limited has a large team, all of whom are either/ both highly qualified in the vocation/ industry area in which they operate on our behalf and/ or are highly qualified Assessors/ Tutors/ Quality Assurance Co-ordinators.

Heavenlyz work leads us to visit many animal care facilities, including grooming salons. Animal Groomers tend to be owners or employees of small businesses. I personally know the struggles of being a student and a business proprietor. My early career as a trainee veterinary nurse allowed me to work in several well respected veterinary practices throughout the Midlands. With help from my family, friends and business partners, I've started up, grown and transferred several successful animal care businesses and I continue to provide consultation services, both to new start up and existing businesses.

Animal Groomers also tend to be people who must juggle busy lives – significant periods of my early businesses were spent with a baby strapped to my back or dealing with the demands of a toddler – for those of you in that or a similar position now, I know how it feels and I commend you.

We're passionate about animals, comfortable not only with dogs and cats but with many species, whether domestic or wild. I spent significant time working for the RSPCA as a shelter's animal care nurse/ shift manager.

We're also passionate about education, throughout our lives. I believe that some of the best times in life are when you can learn something new. I'm not one for resting on my laurels – there is always more to learn and, in all of us, there is always room for improvement. After all these years of working in the Animal Care industry, one of the best feelings I still get is when I attend a seminar where someone is presenting an innovation and can walk away from that presentation richer in knowledge.

This book is designed to provide dog groomers, whether student or experienced, with good, basic, theoretical knowledge. Whether you wish to excel in studies, assessments/ tests OR flourish in your working lives OR just have a good read and learn something new, this book is for you. This manual specifically focusses on the theory required to own, manage or work in a dog grooming salon and its content is relevant to the following specific qualifications: - OCN Dog Grooming Diploma; City & Guilds 7763-02 Level 2 Certificate for Dog Grooming Assistants; City & Guilds 7763-03 Level 3 Introductory Certificate in Dog Grooming; City & Guilds 7863-03 Level 3 Diploma in Dog Grooming.

I'd like to thank all those who have contributed to the book, whether with ideas, knowledge, pictures or other content. I hope you enjoy reading, learning and using the information that is provided on the following pages, I wish you all the very best in your studies, your work and your life and I hope that one day we can meet and discuss our common passion for animals☺.

2 Examination Preparation

If you're reading this book, you've taken the first best step in your exam preparation.

2.1 Revision

Revise, revise, revise – that's the key. Tedious though it may be, committing yourself to repeatedly work through learning materials will help embed knowledge.

Try and start revision almost from the first point of learning, break revision down into chunks, have a plan such that you don't end up cramming. Last minute cramming is much less effective than carefully observed revision time.

Remember that revision is rehearsal. Sometimes, what can be achieve when doing something may not be as good as outcomes during rehearsal – so aim high during rehearsal to compensate for any negatives during the examination itself.

Regards negatives, the more you rehearse/ mentally playback what you expect during the examination the more you are likely to mitigate those negatives. Remember also, though human nature is to feel uneasy/ nervous during times of examination, if you can do so then decide not to be nervous (I know, that's easier said than done...but it is a good aim 😊).

Try and make revision fun. We remember more when we're motivated, enjoying the experience and can relate what we're learning to specific, positive memories.

Ensure your revision environment is appropriate to you – most find that silence aids concentration, but some people need some background noise (hint: a nightclub may not be the best place to revise...BUT, if you're there, with or without fellow students, and you find yourself mentally rehearsing the exam in time to your favourite music, then let it flow 😊).

Don't become a revision hermit. Spend time revising but consider the problems of letting it take over your life. Variety, in all things, stimulates our brains and will lead to better revision outcomes.

Repeat, repeat, repeat – studying something once will help a little, studying something repeatedly, especially when revisited after a period of other activity will help more.

If possible, write it down or type it up – reading is great, but writing/ typing will help your brain make an association between the activity and the content.

Summarise – take content and reduce it to the key points you want to carry with you. This book is written to be as enjoyable a read as it can be, there is no expectation for the student to be able to recite the entire content word for word (tell me if you can, I may have a job for you 😊). Consider making flashcards (brief keynotes on a card summarising a specific topic), especially if you can take these with you (and get them out at parties to wow your friends 😊). Consider also inventing abbreviations or phrases that will help you remember groups of concepts.

Clarify – if you don't understand a word or a phrase, then look it up. If you don't understand the content, carry out your own research.

Self-test – test yourself, or even better get someone else to test you. Ask them to randomise the order of questions, because that's what is likely to happen during any theory exam. Try getting hold of past papers or make your own.

Consider revising with a student undertaking the same qualification or sign up to the Heavenlyz theory revision course.

Consider one last thing – we all learn throughout life, whether we are aware that's happening or not. Committed revision helps us to be better learners and can lead to greater success (however that is personally measured) throughout life.

2.2 Measurements

Some examination materials in the UK still include for imperial measurements. Although this book primarily focusses on metric measurements, students should familiarise themselves with equivalent imperial values or methods to convert from metric to imperial (and imperial to metric) – this may be especially useful to students undertaking exams.

Tel: 01283 703043 Email: liza@heavenlyz.com

2.3 Special Needs

If you have been formally diagnosed with special needs or disability(ies), then disclose these to all parties involved in providing your qualification.

Proof of special needs/ disability(ies) may entitle students (depending on the need/ disability) to extended examination time or other arrangements to the benefit of the student.

Proof constitutes a recent, formal letter of diagnosis from a recognised, independent professional, writing in their professional capacity (i.e. not as an individual, but on letterhead reflecting an entity specialising in the special need/ disability).

When submitting proof, there must be opportunity for corroboration – i.e. those involved in providing the qualification are likely to contact the professional providing the proof for confirmation.

It is up to the student to provide proof of these special needs/ disability(ies) to all those involved in providing the qualification significantly in advance of any examination to guarantee fair access to the examination.

N.B. Many qualification awarding organisations will only accept letters from relevant, suitably qualified medical consultants – those involved in providing the qualification may also have to adhere to the same requirement.

2.4 The Invigilator

For any exam, there will be an invigilator. Their role will include: -

- Room setup/ teardown
- Ensuring the environment is appropriate
- Supporting you throughout the exam
- Prevention of cheating and exclusion of students found to be undertaking this activity
- Exclusion of disruptive students
- Providing clarity as to when the exam starts and finishes (i.e. the period between which the student is under exam conditions)
- Potentially providing clarity as to timings during the examination (if the relevant examination guidelines allow this)

Invigilators are provided to help students, they are not there to assess for student performance.

2.5 Examination structure

Examinations are normally of a fixed duration (i.e. you have limited time).

You may have 1 or more papers to sit in any one exam, they may occur at a time to suit you or you may be restricted to certain dates for the exam.

Exams may be undertaken with pen and paper or they may be undertaken at a computer or tablet.

The structure of the examination will be made clear to the student in advance and is likely to be either: -

- Multiple choice – a limited number of answers, examinees may be required to choose 1 or more correct answers
- Open, short, written answer – written or typed brief answers
- Open long answer written – written or typed longer answers, potentially essays

2.6 Examination techniques

To be comfortable entering the exam, try and understand in advance how many questions there will be in the exam, whether they are of equal weight, what the pass mark is, whether the pass mark is achieved per paper or across multiple papers, whether the exam/ paper pass mark is independent of or combined with any other examination element (e.g. practical assessment) to provide an overall grade.

Get an understanding of how long the examination process will take – compare that to the number of questions and the weight of each question to calculate how much time you should spend on each question, for example: -

Tel: 01283 703043 Email: liza@heavenlyz.com

- A paper has 10 multiple choice questions, they are of equal weight and the student has 30 minutes to complete the exam – this suggests the student should plan to spend 3 minutes maximum on each question (dependant on the knowledge required, 3 minutes is a relatively long time). This is a common type of exam and has probably been designed to give students twice the amount of time normally required to complete the exam.
- A paper has 5 long answer questions, the first three questions are each worth 30% of the overall marks, the last 2 questions are each worth 5% of the overall mark and the student is given 1 hour to complete the exam. This suggests that the student should plan to spend a maximum of 18 minutes for each of the first 3 questions and only 3 minutes on each of the last 2 questions. This type of exam is less common.
- A paper has 180 multiple choice questions, they are of equal weight and the student has 30 minutes to complete the exam – this suggests the student should plan to spend 10 seconds maximum on each question. This examination may be looking for quick reaction, the answers shouldn't require a lot of processing – on the other hand, the exam may be designed to be impossible to finish and the awarding organisation is looking for the strongest candidates who can get closest to completion. This is a rare type of exam

Keep the exam plan flexible – i.e. in the above scenarios, if questions are completed in much less than the maximum time given, then one of two things could be happening. Either, you've not prepared correctly/ misunderstood the instruction and need to adjust OR you're doing well and building yourself a contingency in which you can go back and review the answers previously given.

Not always but usually, the first answer that comes to mind is the correct (or most correct) answer. It is entirely valid to question yourself, especially when you have worked through an entire list of questions and you still have time to start over and review the answers already given. However, if you decide to change an existing answer, then do so carefully and understand your own compelling rationale for changing that answer.

Understand and follow any instructions carefully.

2.7 Multiple Choice Examinations

If multiple-choice and the student cannot identify the right answer, the student should try to eliminate the wrong answers first.

Even then, don't leave any multiple-choice question unanswered. Answer every question, even if it's a guess.

2.8 Open-answer Examinations

Open answer questions can require varying levels of text. Whether hand or type written, they can be tiring, and students should acclimatise themselves to writing/ typing open answers, as if under exam conditions, during revision.

If an essay is required, then have a plan for that essay including an introduction, a more detailed body of investigation – including any position being proposed/ references to other material if necessary – and finally a conclusion.

Write in your own words – even if you have a photographic memory, do not plagiarise ("copy") the work of others (again, students are fully entitled to reference the work of others, BUT references should not take up most of your argument).

Don't waffle 😉. Be precise in your answers, provide clarity, avoid contradicting yourself, build logically to your conclusion.

2.9 Computer based vs written exams

Modern examinations can be carried out either on computer or paper – in either case clear instructions should be provided, but it is worth understanding which format will be in use and to be comfortable with that format (e.g. if you're not computer literate, it will be beneficial to work towards becoming so during your training and revision).

Computer based exams can present most of (or even the entire) subject matter content that you are expected to know, OR they can randomise a subset of questions from a much larger bank of questions held by the examining body (in the latter case, students undertaking the same exam – even on the same day – may not get the same questions).

Tel: 01283 703043 Email: liza@heavenlyz.com

2.10 Attitude

Normally, the best outcome is served where the student is relaxed and focussed. There are several things that can help this: -

- DO prepare well
- DON'T cram throughout the previous night with little or no sleep
- DO sleep and eat well throughout the revision period and especially leading up to the exam
- DO enter the exam with a positive and relaxed attitude
- DO treat your body well, including being careful what you consume and do try to take exercise – "healthy body, healthy mind" is not just an old saying
- AVOID scheduling the exam the morning after a party/ stag/ hen/ your own wedding/ at any other time when you may be affected by unrelated appointments prior or post the exam 😉

2.11 Perspective

What happens if you don't pass?

Well, assuming there haven't been a significant number of attempts, habitually the student gets to repeat the attempt, but there may be a limitation on how soon that repeat can occur and there may be a repeat cost.

But, it is NOT the end of the world, life goes on – it's just a bump in your otherwise wonderful journey 😉.

Tel: 01283 703043 Email: liza@heavenlyz.com

3 Legislation

Although it may initially appear counter-intuitive to Animal Care, the best place we can start is to describe the legislation that protects/ governs all animals (including humans 😉) in the workplace.

Note that legislation relating to animals and businesses is extensive and varies by region – i.e. there are laws in England & Wales that do not apply in Scotland, nor Northern Ireland, and the opposite is also true. There are also areas of law that is left to the interpretation of geographic regions (e.g. boarding kennel license conditions are the domain of local councils).

The remainder of this section summarises legislation applying to England & Wales and doesn't necessarily consider interpretation by geographic regions (i.e. national England & Wales law applies below).

Students and businesses operating in other jurisdictions should still consider the information provided below, and apply it to any assessment/ examination for the qualification being pursued but should also investigate and adhere to jurisdiction as it applies to their own area of operation

We will prioritise with respect to England and Wales for the following reasons: -

- It would be counter-productive to explore all regulation in detail in this book (i.e. the book would contain a significant amount of content not directly relevant to its purpose)
- Most Awarding Organisations issuing qualifications underpinned by this book, do so in England & Wales and define their qualification content against the law of England & Wales.
- A significant amount of legislation in England is mirrored by similar or parallel legislation in Scotland, Wales and Northern Ireland

Readers of this book, students and business owners/ operators are not expected to be, or become, lawyers. However, for all legal requirements, it is in the readers interest to gain an adequate understanding and critically, to always adhere/ not contravene (not "break") the law.

This especially applies to business owners/ operators, whether start-up or existing, where there is a duty of care to staff, customers, service providers and other living beings encountering that business.

Final note – this section concentrates on the major laws applying on or after the date of publication of this book. We neither intend to cover expired laws nor laws that remain active but that only apply to historical agreements (e.g. if a current and relevant law only applies to an agreement made in the past, we do not consider it here).

The main 4 items of animal legislation, to which animal carers are required to adhere, are: -

- Animal Welfare Act 2006 (includes five animal needs)
- Veterinary Surgeon Act 1966
- Clean Neighbourhood and Environmental Act 2005
- Dangerous Dogs Act 1991 (Amended 2014)

Additional legislation that animal care businesses may fall under if they offer other services (e.g. day boarding) includes, but is not limited to, the following: -

- Dogs Act 1871
- Pet Animal Act 1951
- Zoonoses Order 1989
- Animal Boarding Establishment Act 1963, including any local council Home Boarding Establishment Licence Conditions
- Micro-chipping of Dogs Regulation (England) 2015
- Veterinary Medicines Regulations 2013
- Breeding of Dogs Act 1973
- Welfare of Animals (Transport) (England) Order 2006

Further, there are also areas of legislation which are common to any business and to which, again, animal care businesses must adhere: -

Tel: 01283 703043 Email: liza@heavenlyz.com

- Health And Safety At Work Act 1974
- Health And Safety At Work Regulations 1981
- Workplace (Health, Safety And Welfare Regulations) 1992
- Electricity at Work Regulations 1989
- Waste Electrical and Electronic Equipment Regulations 2013 (WEEE)
- The Waste Duty of Care Code of Practice (falls under the EPA 1990)
- Provisions and Use Of Work Equipment Regulations 1998
- Manual Handling Operations Regulations 1992
- Environmental Protection Act (EPA) 1990
- Controlled Waste Regulations 2012
- Control Of Substances Hazardous To Health Regulations 2002 (COSHH)
- Personal Protective Equipment (PPE) Regulations 2002
- Reporting of Injuries, Disease and Dangerous Occurrences Regulations 2013
- Regulatory Reform (Fire Safety) Order 2005
- Equality Act 2010
- Disability Discrimination Act 2005 (Originally 1995)
- Employers' Liability (Compulsory Insurance) Act
- Data Protection Act 1998
- Companies Act 2006 (applies to Limited Companies – and similar legal entities but not Sole Traders)
- National Minimum Wage Act 1998 (predominantly for those who employ others)
- Working Time Regulations 1998
- Work based pensions (2016)
- Employment Act 2010
- Employment Rights Act 1996
- Consumer Rights Act 2015
- Consumer Credit Act 2006
- Supply of Goods (Implied Terms) Act 1973
- Unfair Contract Terms Act 1977
- Supply of Goods and Services Act 1982
- Consumer Protection Act 1987
- Unfair Terms in Consumer Contracts Regulations 1999
- Consumer Protection (Distance Selling) Regulations 2000
- Electronic Commerce Regulations 2002
- Enterprise Act 2002
- Sale and Supply of Goods to Consumers Regulations 2002/3045
- General Product Safety Regulations 2005

As well as understanding current animal welfare legislation, professional animal carers are also required to have a thorough understanding of the following: -

- Public and Employers' liability insurance
- Pay as you earn (PAYE)

Tel: 01283 703043 Email: liza@heavenlyz.com

- Formulation of payslips
- Being a Sole Trader vs. Being a Limited Company (or other, similar, limited liability legal entity)
- Employer's National Insurance Contributions (NICs)

There are also areas for which the UK government publish requirements via the very helpful website "GOV.UK". Note that although GOV.UK is a very good source of information that protects us all, we are ultimately governed by appropriate – normally geographical – jurisdiction. That is, we are NOT ultimately governed by the information on GOV.UK.

The following sections **summarise** legislation as it applies to this industry. If in doubt, http://www.legislation.gov.uk, local authority, industry or legal sources should be consulted before acting. The onus is on the individual (not law enforcement officers) to ensure they, and any legal entity they represent (e.g. a business), comply always with relevant regulations.

Let's start with safeguarding life of all the animals involved. Specifically, UK Law requires that: -

- All people should have a safe place to work
- Animal care related businesses have a duty to ensure that the welfare of animals under care is maintained throughout that care

3.1 Animal Welfare Act 2006

This act places a duty of care on all persons either permanently or temporary caring for an animal to ensure as reasonably as possible the health, safety and welfare of that animals always.

Known as the Five Animal needs;

- The need for a suitable environment
- The need for a suitable diet
- The need to exhibit normal behaviour patterns
- The need to be housed with, or apart from, other animals
- The need to be protected from pain, injury, suffering and disease

We can meet the Five Animal Needs in a salon environment by ensuring that:

- We provide clean and suitable holding units; bedding and we control environmental temperature (i.e. warm in winter and cool in summer)
- We provide fresh water available always
- We provide adequate toilet breaks, space to move and create a relaxed environment alleviating fear or anxiety.
- We ensure all animals are housed individually
- We ensure our animal care areas are clean
- We follow hygiene procedures to avoid cross contamination
- We ensure our animal care areas remain safe (e.g. by ensuring regular PAT testing etc.).

A good reference guide that helps individuals comply with the Animal Welfare Act is called the "Code of Practice for the Welfare of Dogs" and at the time of writing is downloadable from the GOV.UK website.

3.2 Veterinary Surgeons Act 1966

Only a registered Veterinary Surgeons may offer advice on the treatment of animals. This includes diagnosis, diagnostic tests and medical intervention for sick and injured animals. Animal carers are however permitted to deliver emergency first aid but only to alleviate suffering/ prevent condition worsening.

3.3 Clean Neighbourhood and Environmental Act 2005

Part of this act refers to the Dog Control Order relating to the following;

- Fouling of land by dogs and the removal of faeces ("clinical waste")
- The keeping of dogs on leads

Tel: 01283 703043 Email: liza@heavenlyz.com

- The exclusion of dogs on land
- The number of dogs a person may take onto land

Animal carers are advised to display a polite notice, visible outside any premises on which animal care is carried out, requesting that clients be mindful of neighbouring business and homes.

This act also requires that dog owners and handlers clean up the mess left by dogs in their care. This means that, if you are responsible for a dog and it litters outside your premises, you are legally bound to clean the area.

Further, it is important that, animal carers check around any premises in use daily, to avoid negative associations with littering. This is at least advisable from a public relations perspective and will help build good relationships with your neighbours, both private residential and business proprietors, local authorities and passers-by.

3.4 Dangerous Dogs Act 1991 (Amended 2014)

The Dangerous Dogs Act 1991, in brief, currently applies as follows: -

- All dogs will be under proper control in a public place or private household
- If in breach of the dangerous dogs' act, maximum sentence apply as follows: -
    - 14 years if a person dies because of being injured;
    - 5 years in any other case where a person is injured;
    - 3 years in any case where an assistance dog is injured (whether or not it dies).
- A constable or an officer of a local authority authorised by it to exercise the powers conferred by this subsection may seize any dog in a place in England or Wales which is not a public place, if the dog appears to the constable or officer to be dangerously out of control.
- Dangerous Dogs Act 1991 breeds banned are as follows: -
    - Pit Bull Terrier
    - Japanese Tosa
    - Dogo Argentino
    - Fila Brasileiro

Under section 2 of the 1871 Dogs Act, any breed of dog may be reported to the police or a Magistrate's court for acting dangerously and/or out of control. If the court concurs, an order can be made for the dog to be kept by the owner under proper control, or destroyed if an offence is committed.

Increasingly, certain businesses (e.g. pet insurance company) use an expanded version of the list above to exclude full and cross bred breeds of this type from their services.

3.5 Dogs Act 1871

This act relates to the seizure of dogs that are deemed dangerous and not under proper control by a constable in a public place. Once the dog is seized the owner would be notified that the dog is seized and if, after five days of non-collection the dog may be sold or destroyed.

All costs incurred during this process may be payable by the dog owner, the dog owner may be required to go to court and if the dog is returned to the dog owner a court order may be imposed.

This act relates very closely to the Dangerous Dogs Act 1991.

3.6 Pet Animal Act 1951

The Pet Animal Act 1951 applies to the licensing of pet shops and can be summarised as follows: -

- A local authority is responsible for the Licensing of pet shops.
- No person shall keep a pet shop except under the authority of a licence granted in accordance with the provisions of this Act.
- The act also enforces the following: -

Tel: 01283 703043 Email: liza@heavenlyz.com

- Pets not to be sold in streets or on market stalls
- Pets not to be sold to children under twelve years of age.

The local authority has a legal right to inspect any property with a Licence and if a conviction is made under the act, then the court may cancel any licence held, and may (whether the perpetrator is the holder of such a licence) disqualify the license holder from keeping a pet shop for such period as the court thinks fit.

3.7 Zoonoses order 1989

A Zoonotic disease is defined as a disease or infection transmitted from a vertebrate animal to a human. "Zoonoses" (or the less regularly used "Zoonotics") is the collective term for zoonotic diseases.

Transmission of such diseases can be made either by direct exposure (e.g. visiting a farm or pet shop) or by indirect exposure (e.g. consuming contaminated food or drink).

Not all Zoonoses are notifiable. It is advised that a risk assessment be conducted to evaluate the risks of Zoonoses common to the grooming environment to manage health and wellbeing of all who work within that environment. The best primary defence against Zoonotic diseases is proper hand washing, good housekeeping and the provision of PPE.

3.8 Animal Boarding Establishment Act 1963

The following summarises the generic conditions applicable to either a boarding kennels, day care service, breeding bitches and home boarding as follows: -

- Dogs are kept in accommodation suitable in respect of construction, size, temperature, lighting, ventilation and cleanliness.
- The animals are kept secure.
- Reasonable precautions are taken to prevent the spread of infectious disease.
- Appropriate steps are taken in the event of an emergency.
- A suitable, consistent, level of management is maintained.
- There shall be adequate space, light, heat and ventilation for the permitted number of dogs boarded in the day care centre facility at any one time.
- Current vaccination certificates must be presented for each animal on arrival and original certificate retained.
- Dogs must be vaccinated against Canine Distemper, Infectious Canine Hepatitis, Canine Adenovirus, Bordetella Kennel Cough, Leptospirosis and Canine Parvovirus.
- The Licensee must be registered with a veterinary practice that has provided confirmation in writing that facilities will be made available at the premises in the event of an outbreak of infection.
- There must be provided within the grounds of the facility an outdoor area that is securely fenced to prevent escape and that can be used to exercise dogs. This area should be kept clean and faeces shall be removed at least twice a day.
- The Licensee shall ensure that all waste connected with the establishment is disposed of appropriately.
- A copy of the Local Authority Licence must be suitably displayed to the public in a prominent position together with public and employer liability insurance.
- All dogs must have adequate daily exercise
- The perimeter should be paved or surfaced with a suitable material.
- The accommodation and ancillary buildings must be maintained in a state of cleanliness conducive to maintained health and control of disease.
- Animals must be adequately supplied with suitable food if required and must have an adequate supply of wholesome water
- Fresh meat, open tins and all bulk supplies of food must be kept in rat and mouse proof containers.
- All animals must be provided with a bedding area suitable enough to allow the animal to lie comfortably.

- A register must be kept containing a description of any animal received into the establishment to include date of arrival and departure, name and address of owner, etc.
- Appropriate steps must be taken for the protection of animals in case of fire or other emergencies.
- Appropriate Fire Fighting equipment must be provided, and an evacuation procedure must be put in place.
- Licensees shall ensure that a fire risk assessment is regularly undertaken.
- All reasonable precautions should be taken to prevent illegal access to, or escape of, an animal.
- Washing and lavatory facilities must be available for staff.
- A fit and proper person must always be present to exercise/ supervise animals and deal with emergencies

3.8.1 Dedicated Kennels and Catteries

Some animal carers may run associated businesses such as a dog day care facility, cattery or kennel.

Under the provisions of the Animal Boarding Establishments Act 1963, an annual licence may be required to operate a dog day care facility, breeding kennels, home boarding facility and boarding kennels/ cattery.

Government licences are issued/ managed on a regional/ local governmental authority basis and can stipulate many conditions.

New applications for such businesses may involve an inspection, in some cases carried out with a veterinary inspector. Applications normally incur fees and are normally required to be renewed annually – with an annual fee payable. The local authority conducting the inspection will lay out conditions subject to the licence being granted such as: -

- The maximum numbers of dogs permitted in a day
- The requirement for owners to give written consent if their dog is to be boarded together with dogs from other households

3.8.2 Doggy Day Care Centres

These are essentially a crèche for dogs, where owners drop them off, and collect them later in the day. The dogs do not stay overnight. These types of premises are **<u>not</u>** exempt from the Animal Boarding Establishment Act. If you would like to operate a day care centre for dogs in your area, then you will need to consult your local authority and an application for a license may be required.

3.8.3 Home Boarding Establishments

The following Licence Conditions are typical of those covering Home Boarding Establishments: -

- The licence will permit a maximum number of dogs that shall be permitted to be boarded in the residential property at any one time.
- Only dogs from one household may be boarded together at the same time without written consent from owners.
- Dogs boarded at the residential property shall live in the home as family pets.
- No dog boarded in the residential property shall have access to any heater with a direct flame or be left alone in a room that has accessible trailing wires and cables.
- There shall be no use of any free-standing gas or oil appliances whilst there are dogs boarded in the residential property.
- No dog boarded in the residential property shall be left unattended for more than 4 hours.
- If dogs from different households are boarded together, they shall be separated for the duration of any absence of the licensee.
- The licensee shall appoint a responsible person residing within reasonable distance of the premises to have custody of a duplicate key.
- The name, address and telephone number of such a responsible person shall be displayed in legible characters at the front of the premises.
- Generic conditions apply as listed for dog day care crèche and breeding facilities.

Tel: 01283 703043 Email: liza@heavenlyz.com

3.9 Microchipping of Dogs Regulation (England) 2015

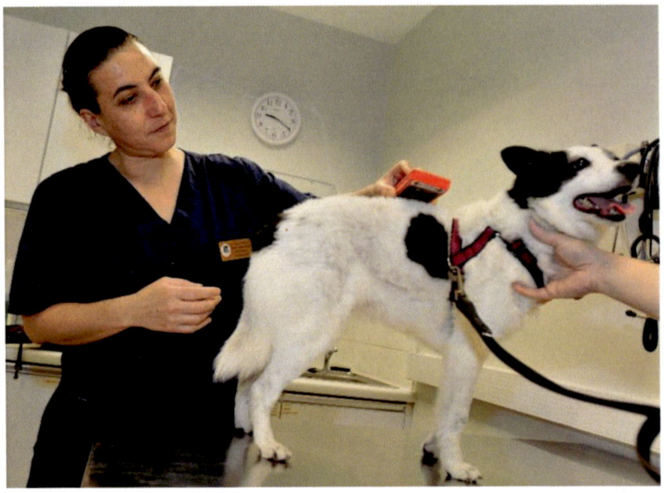

From the 6th April 2016 in England it became compulsory for all dogs over the age of 8 weeks to be microchipped. A microchip is a permanent method of electronic identification.

In the case of dogs, it is about the size of a grain of rice and is inserted subcutaneously (under the skin) between the shoulder blades at the back of the animal's neck.

The procedure is quick, safe and causes little discomfort to the animal. The microchip contains a unique number that is then entered onto a database of information that has information about the dog and the owner.

Once the microchip is implanted into an animal it can be read by a microchip scanner, a non-invasive scanning device that quickly reads the chip through the skin of the animal and can identify the number stored on the chip.

Where a dog is transferred to a different owner, the new owner is responsible for updating the database (informing the company to which the dog is microchipped with) of their new address, full name and contact telephone number.

All owners are also required to ensure the database is always kept up to date of the owner details.

Failure to have your dog microchipped could result in the owner being fined and/or the dog not being returned if it should get lost or be stolen.

Only certain people are permitted to implant microchips: -

- a veterinary surgeon
- a veterinary nurse (under veterinary surgeon supervision) either student or qualified
- a person who has attended (and been satisfactorily assessed on) an approved training course

Any person implanting microchips that does not fall under the categories specified is committing an offence.

3.10 Veterinary Medicines Regulations 2013

This legislation is enforced in the UK and controls medicines that are used or designed for use by animals. It covers the manufacture, advertising, supply, administration, possession, classification and importation of such medicines.

A Veterinary Medicinal Product (VMP) is defined as any substance presented as having properties for treating or preventing diseases in animals.

The legislation is very detailed and covers all aspects of the way in which veterinary medicine are controlled including the intended use of medicines, how they are advertised, the labelling requirements, prescription requirements, data storage, and the use of authorised and unauthorised medicines. It also looks at the way in which certain types of products are advertised and the wording that can be used for certain products.

A person would be guilty of an offence if they do not comply with some ore more of sections of this legislation and they may be liable to a fine or imprisonment.

It is advisable that if you a providing an animal care service for an animal that requires medication that you ensure that you have the following in place: -

- Container clearly labelled with: animal, vet and owner details; dosage amounts and intervals
- Ensure sufficient medicine in container for dose required
- Store medication out of reach of other animals and ensure that only the animal named receives the medicine
- Do not put medicine in shared feeding bowls or areas
- Keep clear records of medication given and observe for any unexpected side effects after given

Tel: 01283 703043 Email: liza@heavenlyz.com

3.11 Breeding of Dogs Act 1973

The 1973 Breeding of Dogs Act requires proprietors of breeding establishments to be licensed annually. The licence stipulates the conditions which must be complied with by the licensee. The aim of the licensing system is to ensure that high standards of animal welfare are maintained. The following is a summary list of conditions that comprise the 1973 Breeding of Dogs Act: -

- The licence will outline the maximum number of breeding bitches kept at the premises
- Bitches that are less than one year old shall not be mated
- Bitches shall not give birth to more than six litters of puppies each in a lifetime
- Bitches shall not give birth to puppies before the end of the period of twelve months beginning with the day on which they gave birth to puppies
- Generic conditions apply as listed for dog day care crèche and breeding facilities.

3.12 The Welfare of Animals (Transport) (England) Order 2006

Transport of Animals is regulated through the Welfare of Animals (Transport), Order 2006 ("WATEO 2006"). In addition to this legislation, there also exist the following 2 pieces of legislation most relevant to transportation of animals of which an awareness is recommended: -

- **DEFRA (the Government Department for Environment, Food and Rural Affairs) briefly stipulate that all animals should: -**
    - Have rest, water and food as necessary throughout the journey
    - NOT be transported if the journey is likely to cause distress or injury
    - Be transported by personnel fully trained in the transportation of animals
    - Be fit to travel and have their journeys properly planned
    - Be provided with suitable vehicle restraints (e.g. cages are suitable for the pet)
- **The Highway Code also states that pets will be suitably restrained so they cannot distract the driver or injure themselves - this means pets should NEVER be transported loose.**

3.13 Health and Safety at Work Act(s)

UK Legislation places a duty of care on all employers to ensure as reasonably possible the health safety and welfare at work of all those affected by the operations of the business. The Act, originating in 1974 has been through many revisions and fundamentally requires: -

- Safe operation and maintenance of the working environment
- Maintenance of safe access to the workplace
- Safe use, handling and storage of dangerous substances
- Adequate training of staff to ensure health and safety
- Adequate welfare provisions for staff at work
- Maintenance of a written record of health and safety policies (applicable where there are 5 or more employees)

An 'in house written' health and safety policy or the HSE Poster should be displayed prominently to which all salon personnel can clearly refer. Ensure all staff have had an induction to the work place, received correct ongoing training and understand their own responsibilities and how their behaviour could impact on the workplace.

Regardless whether self-employed, sole trader or working within a small team, UK law requires that illnesses or injuries caused through work are recorded. All employers must ensure employees who become ill or injure themselves at work receive immediate attention, including calling an ambulance (dial 999) in serious cases.

Tel: 01283 703043 Email: liza@heavenlyz.com

The employer should assess the hazards and risks in your workplace and establish an appropriate level of first-aid provision.

The trained First Aid person or persons' names should be displayed, and all staff and visitors made aware of whom they are. Note that the First Aid station can be clearly recognised by a white cross on a green background, all first aid equipment should be in date, easily accessible and should be located within areas of the workplace where it may be required.

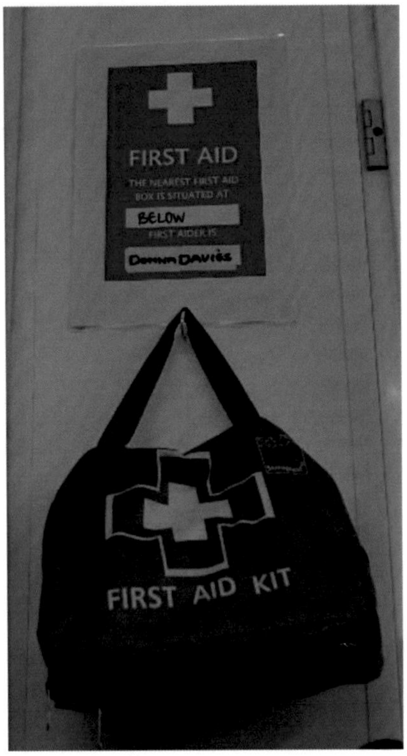

Employers are required to maintain a healthy work environment, maintain safety and welfare of employees to include employee-friendly control of: -

- Workplace environment
- Temperature in indoor workplace
- Ventilation
- Lighting
- Room dimensions and space
- Suitability of workstation and seating
- Safety: -
    - safe passage of pedestrians
    - windows and sky lights – safe opening, closing, cleaning
    - transparent doors and partitions – use of safety material and markings
    - doors, gates operate safely
    - floors – constructed and maintained including trip and slip hazards
    - prevention falling objects and falling into hazardous substances
- Facilities: -
    - Clean and maintained toilets
    - Clean and maintained eating and changing facilities
    - Clean and maintained clothing storage
    - Clean and maintained rest area, arrangements to protect people from tobacco smoke.
    - Rest area for pregnant mothers and nursing mothers.
- House Keeping
- Maintenance of workplace, equipment and facilities
- Cleanliness
- Removal of waste materials

Additional Health & Safety regulations set out broad general guidelines which apply to almost all kinds of work. They require employers to assess the risks to the health and safety of their employees and anyone else who may be affected by the activity to identify the necessary preventative and protective measures needed to eliminate or significantly reduce the risks.

Tel: 01283 703043 Email: liza@heavenlyz.com

3.14 The Electricity at Work Regulations 1989

These regulations control electrical safety in the workplace. Both employers and employees are required to comply with the regulations.

Electrical wiring and equipment must be sound, properly installed and competently maintained.

Annual Portable Appliance Testing (PAT) is recommended to be carried out annually on all regularly used portable electrical equipment that is not covered by manufacturer's guarantees or is over one year old.

The appliances should be labelled, and a written certificate produced with renewal date recorded.

3.15 Waste Electrical and Electronic Equipment Regulations 2013 (WEEE)

Prior to the implementation of the WEEE directive in the UK, waste electronic and electrical equipment was disposed of in the household (municipal) waste stream. Post the introduction of the Hazardous Waste Regulations Exclusions apply to electrical and electronic equipment that are deemed hazardous. Hazardous electronic wastes comprise: -

- Uninterruptable power supplies, lead-acid batteries
- Cathode ray tubes (televisions, computer monitors)
- Fluorescent tubes, backlights to laptop screens, thin-film transistors
- Electrical/electronic equipment containing polychlorinated biphenyl (PCB)
- Fridges and freezers, due to chlorofluorocarbon (CFC), an ozone-depleting substance. As of 2012 revisions to the regulations, all refrigerants are considered Hazardous.

3.16 Provisions and Use of Work Equipment Regulations 1998

Employers have a duty to consider the health and safety risks when selecting equipment, to make sure the equipment is suitable, and to give employees adequate information, instruction and training.

The regulations also cover the isolation of equipment from power sources and provisions of adequate warnings and markings.

It is good practice, display a clear sign with location of Mains Electric Circuit isolator and ensure all personnel working within the salon have been inducted with its location.

3.17 Manual Handling Operations Regulations 1992

These regulations place a duty on employers to avoid hazardous handling as far as reasonably possible and make a suitable assessment of any manual handling which may be hazardous and yet cannot be avoided. The assessment must be in writing, monitored closely and be revised. Employees are required to comply with the employer and follow set procedures as required.

It is good practice, where financially possible, to invest in a hydraulic table where the height of the table is adjustable. Hydraulic tables allow individual groomers to work at a safe table height and mitigate strain, notably to the back, and especially make handling of larger breeds easier.

3.18 Environmental Protection Act (EPA) 1990

Under section 34 of the EPA, as groomers we have a duty of care to ensure that all waste arising from our premises are disposed of without harm to human health or the environment. Waste should be disposed of by a registered carrier who should transport it to an appropriate licensed or authorised disposal facility. On collection of such waste, a waste transfer note should be provided to you by your chosen carrier.

It is good practice, prior to setting up your salon (regardless of whether from home, mobile or commercial property) to seek the advice of your local authority's Environmental Officer or Heath Department as waste disposal requirements vary from one local authority to another.

Noise emissions also fall into this Act. Adequate planning is required when setting up a salon to consider the problem and prevention of potential noise caused by barking dogs. If you manage an appointment system this will help to minimise dogs waiting around the salon between treatments, reducing stress, anxiety and the consequent potential for noise. It is useful to document dogs who are prone to barking as, usually, there is a trigger for barking. It is good practice to investigate what that trigger may be and to avoid the trigger being apparent in future appointments.

Regards the "Duty of Care Act 1991" referred to in several awarding organisation qualification handbooks. This "Duty of Care Act 1991" is referring to section 34 of the EPA 1990 as well as The Environmental Protection (Duty of Care) Regulations 1991.

3.19 Controlled Waste Regulations 2012

This legislation outlines the types of waste into the following three categories;

1. Industrial waste – industrial waste is defined as waste from manufacturing or industrial processes (that is non-hazardous). Good examples or Industrial Waste are: -

   a) waste generated from aircraft or vehicles,
   b) waste produced by a laboratory,
   c) waste from excavation or tunnelling,
   d) certain types of clinical waste,
   e) certain categories of poisonous or noxious waste,
   f) waste from premises breeding, boarding, stabling or exhibiting animals,
   g) waste from oil or scrap metal handling

2. Commercial waste – commercial waste is defined as waste arising from a trade or business. Good examples of Commercial Waste are waste that is generated from offices, showrooms, hotels, private garages, club/society or from a market/fair.

3. Household waste - household waste is defined as waste that is produced on a domestic property. Good examples of residential waste are: -

   a) waste generated from camp sites, prisons, halls open to public meetings, a Royal palace, a moored vessel,
   b) a private storage facility containing only domestic waste,
   c) waste generated from caravans,
   d) waste generated from residential homes or waste that is derived from a charity or a charitable event. Waste that does not fall under the category of household waste would be scrap metal, mineral, synthetic oil, grease, asbestos and clinical waste.

Under this regulation, your local authority has the right to impose additional residential waste collection charges on the following types of waste; garden waste, dead domestic pets, clinical waste, waste that does not fit into the waste container, waste that is too heavy and asbestos.

This regulation includes an amendment that from 2015 waste collection authorities must collect the following waste separately; glass, paper, metal and plastic.

Tel: 01283 703043 Email: liza@heavenlyz.com

3.20 Control of Substances Hazardous to Health Regulations 2002 (COSHH)

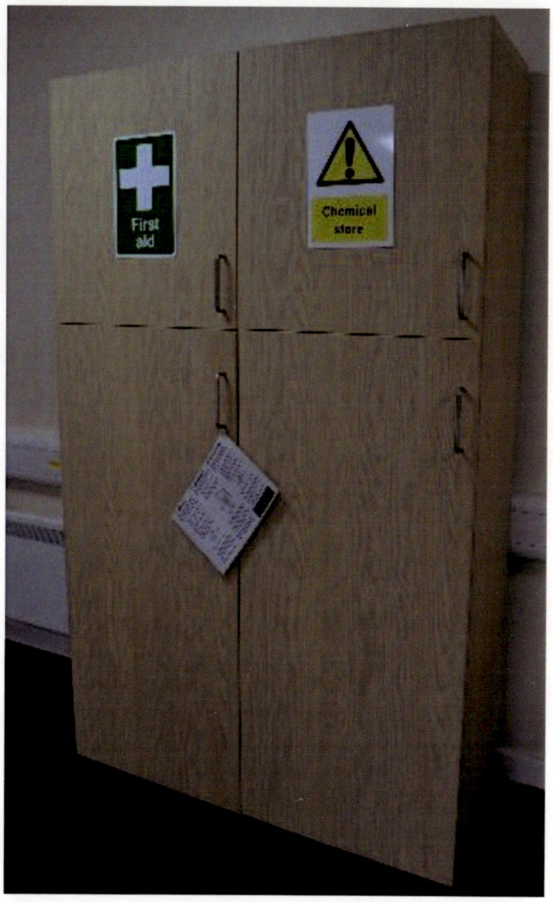

Each business is required to assess activities liable to expose employees to hazardous materials/ hazardous substances/ hazardous chemicals in the work place. For the rest of this section we will refer to all as "substances".

Hazardous substances could harm health if they are not properly controlled. Examples of hazardous substances in the animal care industry are dust, dander, glues, paints, cleaning agents and flammable products such as dog fragrance sprays or oils.

Employers are responsible for assessing risks and controlling exposure of hazardous substances to their employees.

People can be exposed to substances in a variety of ways including ingestion, through skin, through eyes, through skin puncture and through inhalation.

For bought products deemed 'dangerous for supply', the supplier is legally required to provide the consumer with a safety data sheet along with each product. This does not cover pesticides, cosmetics and medicines, covered under separate legislation.

COSHH is all about controlling exposure to hazardous substances, rather than eliminating the substances from the workplace. COSHH places a duty of care on the employer to ensure that all staff are aware of hazardous chemicals, that they are fully trained to safely work with them, that they are provided with adequate, well maintained PPE and where necessary that they are provided with the opportunity for health surveillance.

COSHH also covers Zoonoses (that is diseases that can be transmitted from animals to humans), e.g. Lyme disease spread by infected ticks.

Under COSHH, the employer must regularly assess the risks within the workplace and implement appropriate/ adequate controls. Controls are identified via a formal process called a risk assessment. On new staff induction, introduction of new process/ product or simply a significant change in the workplace, the COSHH Risk assessment should be reviewed and revised if necessary.

3.21 Personal Protective Equipment (PPE) Regulations 2002

This includes most types of equipment such as clothing, eye goggles and ear defenders. Employers have a duty to: -

- Assess risks, maintain, clean and replace all PPE
- Provide storage for PPE
- Ensure PPE is properly used
- Give training, information and instruction on PPE

Suggested best practice if all PPE is easily visible by either having advisory signs displayed or storage area labelled

3.22 Reporting of Injuries, Disease and Dangerous Occurrences Regulations 2013

The Reporting of Injuries, Disease and Dangerous Occurrences Regulations 2013 (RIDDOR) govern the reporting of certain occurrences. Only 'responsible persons' including employers, the self-employed and people in control of work premises should submit reports under RIDDOR. This Regulation Requires the employer to notify RIDDOR of certain injuries, disease and dangerous occurrences for most types of incidents, including: -

Tel: 01283 703043 Email: liza@heavenlyz.com

- accidents resulting in the death of any person
- accidents resulting in specified injuries to workers
- non-fatal accidents requiring hospital treatment to non-workers and dangerous occurrences
- a report must be received within 10 days of the incident.
- For accidents resulting in the over-seven-day incapacitation of a worker, you must notify the enforcing authority within 15 days of the incident, using the appropriate online form.
- Employers have a duty to report any deaths or major injuries.

3.23 Regulatory Reform (Fire Safety) Order 2005

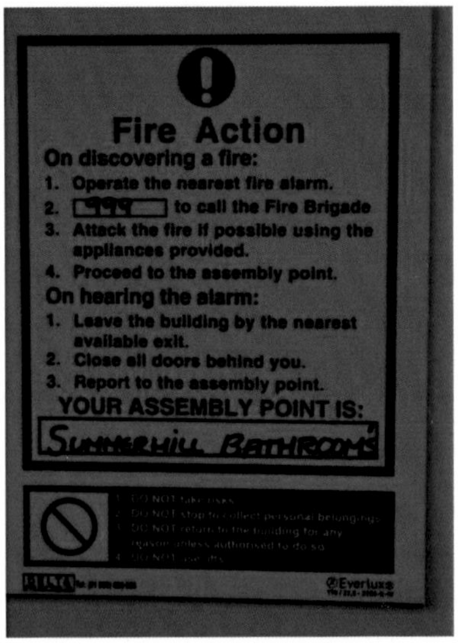

Employers have a duty to implement and maintain a fire management plan. A risk assessment is conducted, and all preventative measures are outlined and implemented. These could include a fire alarm system, extinguishers as well as clearly signed escape routes. A written fire procedure should be in place and all staff and visitors should be made aware of the fire procedures to follow in emergencies.

3.24 Equality Act 2010

This Act is in place to legally protect people from discrimination in the workplace and in the wider society. It protects people from discrimination by means of any of the following nine characteristics: -

1. age
2. being or becoming a transsexual person
3. being married or in a civil partnership
4. being pregnant or on maternity leave
5. disability
6. race including colour, nationality, ethnic or national origin
7. religion, belief or lack of religion/belief
8. sex
9. sexual orientation

Many types of people are protected from discrimination in the following situations; at work, in education, as a consumer, when using public services, when buying or renting property and as a member or guest of a private club or association.

3.25 Disability Discrimination Act 2005 (originally 1995)

The DDA 2005 remains applicable to Northern Ireland only, having been replaced in England, Wales and Scotland by the Equality Act 2010 (see above).

This Act is in place to protect disabled people, or people who have had a disability from discrimination, a disabled person is someone who, at the relevant time: -

- has a physical or mental impairment that has an adverse and substantial effect on their ability to carry out normal day-to-day activities
- the effect of the impairment is long term (has lasted for 12 months, is likely to last for at least that period, or is likely to last the rest of that person's life, or in the case of a past disability, if the effect is likely to be recurrent).

This Act was updated in 2005 so that it now places a duty on all public authorities to have due regard to the need to: promote equality of opportunity between disabled and other persons, eliminate discrimination that is unlawful under the Act, eliminate harassment of disabled persons that is related to their disabilities, promote positive attitudes towards disabled persons in public life, take steps to take account of disabled persons' disabilities, even where that involves treating disabled persons more favourably that other persons.

Tel: 01283 703043 Email: liza@heavenlyz.com

3.26 Employers' Liability (Compulsory Insurance) Act

This act requires employers to hold employers' liability insurance.

The act applies in England, Scotland or Wales from 1969 and there is a separate, similar act applying to Northern Ireland from 1999.

Employer's must take out an insurance policy from an authorised insurer, deemed so by the Financial Conduct Authority (FCA). The minimum level of cover required is £5,000,000.

A valid certificate must be displayed where it can be easily read by employees.

Failure to take out adequate insurance cover can result in serious, business impacting, daily fines.

Failure to make the insurance available for your employees can also result in a significant fine.

Public liability insurance is a different type of insurance and covers a business against members of the public or customers making a claim against them, whereas Employers' liability insurance refers to protecting your business against any claim an employee may make.

Public insurance is not a legal requirement; however, it is recommended for businesses who interact with the public/ customers to have this type of insurance.

3.27 Data Protection Act (DPA) 1998

Any records or data kept in the salon must be protected. If you handle personal information about individuals, you have a legal obligation to protect that information under the Data Protection Act 1998. The Data Protection Act stipulates: -

- Personal Data shall be processed fairly and lawfully
- Personal data shall be obtained only for one or more specified and lawful purpose.
- Personal data shall be adequate, relevant and not excessive
- Personal data shall not be kept for longer than is necessary
- Appropriate measures to ensure personal data is not accidentally lost or unlawfully processed (kept in a lockable facility)
- Personal data shall not be transferred outside the European economic area
- Personal data is required to be stored, and at the appropriate time disposed of, securely

Types of records that need to be kept within the business and their importance: -

- Client information records (n.b. **personal** data)
- Animal/ pet information records
- Client disclaimers (e.g. contract of grooming/ boarding – also likely to contain **personal** data)
- Business Accounts (Income/ Expenditure/ Debtors/ Creditors/ Analyses)
- Health and safety records – highly likely to contain **personal** data)
- Employee records (n.b. **personal** data)
- Human accident records (n.b. **personal** data)
- Animal/ pet accident records

These information records should be maintained according to legal and business requirements (for the avoidance of doubt, legal requirements outweigh business requirements). Storage can be paper or electronic based (e.g. software installed on a computer or an application accessed over the internet).

Any records retained by the business should be kept in an appropriate (locked/ secure) manner. This applies 24hrs per day and throughout the year, whether staff are on or offsite. It is the business's responsibility to ensure that records are always stored securely.

Whether records are stored on paper or electronically, the business should ensure that it adheres to the DPA. This is especially important where records are stored on behalf of the business but by a 3rd party. For example, old records are held in a storage facility on behalf of the business OR the business uses 3rd party software – a booking management system. Even in these cases, the business must assure itself that client

Tel: 01283 703043 Email: liza@heavenlyz.com

understands that it's information will be held by a 3rd party AND that the 3rd party adheres to all aspects of the DPA.

The business must only record client information relevant to the services it is providing now or intends to provide to the client in the future – the business must be able to provide proof that these services are currently provided or to be provided in future.

Records should be retained only for a period required by law or the needs of the business. Where the business ceases to provide services to a client, that client's information should be disposed of correctly or retained securely where the business can prove that retention is necessary.

Where records are required to be disposed, because of the needs of the business and legal requirements (including DPA), disposal should be carried out such that records are totally eradicated. This includes disposal of any copies of records, whether help on paper or electronically. Care should especially be taken regards electronic records where the business or any 3rd party may hold backups of data. At the very least, the business should be able to demonstrate that every care has been taken to dispose of all copies of records and that any repository on which records remain are still secure.

It is the business responsibility to dispose of records correctly. Records can be disposed of in several ways: -

- Paper records may be shredded or given to a professional 3rd party disposal contractor (with whom the business has a contract and who is able to demonstrate adherence to UK legal requirements, including the DPA.
- The records are held electronically in a "naked" format on the business's own repository (i.e. created by the business): -
  - physically (e.g. removal and destruction of hard drives where records – or copies – exist)
  - using any available operating system tools, where that operating system adheres to the DPA
  - using any 3rd party tool, where that 3rd party tool adheres to the DPA
- The records are held electronically in a system or application, either installed on a machine owned by the business or accessed over the internet
  - If the business knows all the places where the system/ application stores records, then physical disposal (as described above) can be considered
  - Using functionality within the 3rd party system/ application that is known to dispose of records as per the requirements of the DPA

Whether stored physically or electronically, the business should consider who has access to these records and at what times that access is permitted. That is, staff of the business should only have access to records appropriate to their role and appropriate to the times within which they work. This requires any records to be secured such that those who may have access to these records do so for a compelling business reason. Liability for staff abuse of records lies both with the staff involved and with the business (because the business failed to properly secure the records).

Special consideration should be made for the following: -

- staff who have access to business premises and any records secured only because of business premise locks
- staff who have access to business records whilst away from the business premises (e.g. remotely, over the internet)
- access to electronic business records remotely by persons unknown to the business (whether because the business has failed to properly secure its data – by firewalls, incorrect system configuration, etc. – or because the person has managed to gain access to the business data by illegal means – e.g. virus's/ worms/ keyloggers).

3.28 General Data Protection Regulation

In May 2018 an EU framework called the General Data Protection Regulation (GDPR) will replace the Data Protection Act (DPA). GDPR has greater scope and much tougher punishments for those who fail to comply with new rules around the storage and handling of personal data.

While this new framework comes into place as the UK is undergoing BREXIT, the UK's Great Repeal Act means that GPDR is likely to be converted into British law.

One of the biggest GPDR changes concerns consent. Under GPDR, companies must keep a thorough record of how and when an individual gives consent to store and use their personal data.

Consent will mean active agreement. Companies can no longer infer consent, they will have to hold explicit permission from customers. Companies will have to show a clear audit trail of consent (e.g. saved consent forms).

Individuals will have the right to withdraw consent at any time, easily and swiftly. When somebody does withdraw consent, their details must be permanently erased. GDPR gives individuals the right to be forgotten.

In the event of a data breach, GDPR forces companies to inform relevant authorities within 72 hours, giving full details of the breach and proposals for mitigating its effects.

GDPR forces SMEs to know exactly what personal data they hold and where it is located (whether on PCs, on servers, or the internet), and have procedures in place to ensure complete removal of data on request. Protocols must be available to monitor, recognise and act on breaches as soon as they happen, and an incident recovery plan must be put in place to deal with any possible repercussions.

3.29 Companies Act 2006 (applies to Limited Companies – and similar legal entities but not Sole Traders)

The Companies Act contains various provisions which affect all companies irrespective of their status. It governs several items, including: -

- Company formation, including the procedure for incorporating companies
- Constitutional documents that define the company
- Shareholder meetings
- Shareholder communications
- Company Auditor's liability

3.30 National Minimum Wage Act 1998 (predominantly for those who employ others)

This act simply introduces a national minimum wage, applicable against a set of criteria (predominantly age).

3.31 Working Time Regulations 1998

These Regulations govern UK worker's time. They apply to all workers (not just employees) and stipulate minimum rest breaks, daily rest, weekly rest and the maximum average working week. It sets a default rule that workers may work no more than 48 hours per week (although an opt out is available), it provides for a minimum of 4 weeks paid annual leave (including bank holidays and public holidays) and provides a minimum 20-minute rest period in any continuous period of work lasting over 6 hours.

3.32 Work based pensions (2016)

This act requires employers to enrol employees into a workplace pension scheme if the employee: -

- is not already in one, or they've not enrolled you into one
- is aged between 22 and State Pension age
- earns more than £10,000 a year
- usually work in the UK

The employee can opt out if wished, but would then not receive employer and government pension contributions.

3.33 Employment Rights Act 1996

This act governs the fundamentals of employment, including mandating a formal contract of employment, correct dismissal protocols, rights of redundancy and rights to paid time off work.

Tel: 01283 703043 Email: liza@heavenlyz.com

3.34 Consumer Rights Act 2015

The Consumer Rights Act 2015 replaced three major pieces of consumer legislation – the Sale of Goods Act, Unfair Terms in Consumer Contracts Regulations and the Supply of Goods and Services Act. It was introduced to simplify, strengthen and modernise the law, giving consumers' clearer shopping rights.

Under the Consumer Rights Act all products – whether physical or digital/ electronic – must be of satisfactory quality, fit for purpose and as described.

Products must be: -

- Of satisfactory quality – Goods shouldn't be faulty or damaged when you receive them.
- Fit for purpose – the goods should be fit for the purpose they are supplied for, as well as any specific purpose you made known to the retailer before you agreed to buy the goods.
- As described – the goods supplied must match any description given to you, or any models or samples shown to you at the time of purchase.

3.35 Consumer Credit Act 2006

This Act adds powers to credit regulation existing at that time by: -

- providing consumers with the option of using the Financial Ombudsman Service if they are unhappy with their lender's dispute resolution service, whether the lender consents or not. Complaints may also be raised against other types of credit related companies, such as debt-collection agencies.
- increasing the powers of the Office of Fair Trading in relation to consumer credit and permitting borrowers to challenge unfair debtor-creditor relationships in court. It empowers the Office of Fair Trading (OFT) to investigate applicants for consumer credit licences, to impose conditions on licences, and to impose civil penalties of up to £50,000 on companies which fail to comply with its conditions.
- extending regulation to consumer agreements above £25,000 as well as small, one-man businesses and partnerships of up to three people.

3.36 Supply of Goods (Implied Terms) Act 1973

This act provided implied terms in contracts for the supply of goods and for hire-purchase agreements, and limited the use of exclusion clauses.

3.37 Unfair Contract Terms Act 1977

This act regulates contracts by restricting the operation and legality of some contract terms. It extends to nearly all forms of contract and one of its most important functions is limiting the applicability of disclaimers of liability. The terms extend to both actual contract terms and notices that are seen to constitute a contractual obligation.

The Act requires terms excluding or limiting liability ineffective to demonstrate reasonableness, depending on the nature of the obligation to be excluded and whether the party excluding or limiting liability, is a business acting against a consumer.

3.38 Consumer Protection Act 1987

This Act made important changes to UK consumer law. It introduced a regime of strict liability for damage arising from defective products, created government powers to regulate the safety of consumer products through Statutory Instruments and defined a criminal offence of giving a misleading price indication.

3.39 Consumer Contracts (Information, Cancellation and Additional Charges) Regulations 2013

This act requires traders to give consumers certain information on contracts agreed on or after 13th June 2014 (contracts agreed prior to 13 June 2014 are covered by the Distance Selling Regulations).

Application varies depending on whether the sale is made at the trader's premises ("on-premise") or at a distance (e.g. online or phone) or face-to-face but away from the trader's business premises (both the latter are "off-premise").

For distance or off-premises sales, key information which the trader must provide includes: -

Tel: 01283 703043 Email: liza@heavenlyz.com

- a description of the goods, service or digital content, including how long any commitment will last on the part of the consumer
- the total price of the goods, service or digital service or the way the price will be calculated if this can't be determined
- how the consumer will pay for the goods or services and when they will be provided to the consumer
- all additional delivery charges and other costs (and if these charges can't be calculated in advance, the fact that they may be payable)
- details of who pays for the cost of returning items if the consumer have a right to cancel and change the consumer's mind
- details of any right to cancel - the trader also needs to provide, or make available, a standard cancellation form to make cancelling easy (although the consumer isn't under any obligation to use it)
- information about the seller, including their geographical address and contact details and the address and identity of any other trader for whom the trader is acting
- information on the compatibility of digital content with hardware and other software that the trader is aware of (or can reasonably be expected to be aware of).

Failure to provide required information (or to provide it as set out by the regulations), could result in cancellation rights being extended by up to a year.

The information should be provided in writing in a 'durable medium' such as on paper or by email. Alternatively, it can be provided in a way appropriate to the means of communication (e.g. verbal where contract made by phone).

Consumers are also entitled to confirmation of the contract – if the information wasn't initially provided in a durable form, the trader must provide it at the point of confirmation.

For on-premises sales, the trader doesn't have to provide as much information in this instance, but it must still provide certain information (e.g. information about the goods or services being bought, the price, the compatibility of digital content and details of any delivery costs).

3.40 Electronic Commerce Regulations 2002

This act applies to contracts concluded by electronic means over distance where the buyer is a "natural person acting for the purposes other than those of his trade, business or profession."

Before the contract is formed, the seller must state in a "clear comprehensible and unambiguous manner" the technical step involved to place an order (contractual offer). Terms and conditions under which the contract is concluded must be made available to the consumer in a means capable of reproduction and storage.

The seller must provide acknowledgement of the order by electronic means without undue delay as well as information of how to amend any input errors made.

Where the consumer has not been informed in the correct manner of the procedure to amend errors in orders and they have made errors, the contract can be rescinded.

The act provides that a contractual offer occurs when the order is sent, and that the acknowledgement constitutes a contractual acceptance.

3.41 Enterprise Act 2002

This Act had several objectives, including: -

- eradicating forms of anti-competitive behaviour
- provide redress to injured parties where competition is distorted

Essentially, it provides an increased deterrence for forming cartels. The competition commission also had its scope widened to cover investigations of whole industries, not just specific firms.

3.42 General Product Safety Regulations 2005

This act demands that "No producer shall [supply or] place a [consumer] product on the market unless the product is a safe product" and provides for broad enforcement powers.

3.43 Operating as a Sole Trader

A sole trader runs a business as a self-employed individual and keeps all business's profits after the correct tax has been applied.

Sole traders must retain accounting records, but these are not generally required to be audited. Sole traders are personally liable for losses of their business.

There is no specific regulation that governs operating as a sole trader.

Due to the absence of specific sole trader regulation, companies (especially large companies with direct legal representation) may not deal with sole traders.

3.44 Operating as a Limited Company

Directors run a business as self-employed individual and keep all business's profits after the correct tax has been applied.

Directors must retain accounting records and in certain situations these are not required to be audited. Directors have limited liability for losses of their business.

There are specific regulations governing operating as a limited company.

3.45 Employer's National Insurance Contributions (NICs)

"National Insurance Contributions" (NICs) are paid by employees and employers on earnings, and by employers on certain benefits-in-kind provided to employees. The self-employed contribute partly by a fixed weekly or monthly payment, and partly on a percentage of net profits above a certain threshold. Individuals may also make voluntary contributions, to fill a gap in their contributions record and thus protect their entitlement to benefits. Contributions from those in employment are collected by HM Revenue and Customs (HMRC) through the PAYE system, along with Income Tax, repayments of Student Loans and any Apprenticeship Levy which the employer is liable to pay.

3.46 Pay as you earn (PAYE)

The Pay As You Earn (PAYE) system is a method of paying income tax and national insurance contributions. Employers deduct tax and national insurance contributions from employee's wages or occupational pension before paying wage or pension amounts. That is, the employee does not get the gross wage paid into their bank account, employees get a nett amount after deductions (NETT = GROSS – DEDUCTIONS).

Wages includes sick pay, maternity or paternity pay and adoption pay. Employees pay tax via the PAYE system throughout the year, each time the employee is paid, rather than paying in one lump sum.

The employer is responsible for sending the tax on to HM Revenue and Customs (HMRC). Each pay day the employer gives the employee a pay slip describing gross pay, tax, national insurance contributions and any other deductions as well as the nett residual pay. If the employer provides a pension, then the employee may not get a payslip for every payment.

At the end of the tax year, the employee gets a form ("P60") setting out the total amounts paid to and deducted from the employee for the previous tax year (tax years run from 6 April one year to 5 April the following year).

If tax is paid/ deducted from an employee's wages or occupational pension under PAYE, the PAYE system can also be used to collect income tax on any other taxable income received. The PAYE system can also be used to collect tax due on other sources of income such as untaxed interest or rent as well as other money owed to HMRC, such as overpaid tax credits, tax debts from previous years and unpaid self-employed national insurance contributions.

3.47 Formulation of payslips

An employee must be provided with the following information on their payslip: -

- Your personal information
- Your name and sometimes your home address will be shown.
- Your payroll number
- Some companies use payroll numbers to identify individuals on the payroll.

Tel: 01283 703043 Email: liza@heavenlyz.com

- Date - The date your pay should be credited to your bank account is usually shown.
- Tax period - The number here represents the tax period for that payslip, for example if you're paid monthly, 01 = April and 12 = March.
- Your tax code
- Your tax code will be sent to you by HM Revenue & Customs (HMRC).
- The code tells your employer how much tax-free pay you should get before deducting tax from the rest. If the code is wrong, you could end up paying too much or too little tax, so you should check this against your latest your tax code notice.
- Your National Insurance (NI) number
- You must have a NI number to work in the UK.
- You have the same NI number throughout your whole life – even if you change your name.
- It's your personal number for the whole of the social security system. It's used to make sure all your contributions are recorded properly, and helps to build up your entitlement to state benefits – like a pension.
- Payments, wages, bonuses, commission
- This will show how much you have earned in wages before any deductions are made.
- It might also show how your pay was calculated, for example your hourly rate and the number of hours worked.
- It could also show any extra payments you have earned on top of your basic pay like bonuses, commission or overtime.
- Expenses
- Your employer might pay any expenses owed to you via the payroll.
- Some employers will list each expense payment separately on the payslip. Others combine them to show a taxable or non-taxable amount.
- Deductions – tax and National Insurance - Your payslip must show the amount of variable deductions, such as tax and National Insurance.
- Pensions
- If you're paying towards a workplace pension that your company has set up or arranged access to, the amount you're contributing will be shown.
- If your employer is contributing too, that amount might also be shown.
- Student loan
- If you're making repayments on a student loan, this will be shown on your payslip.
- If you're an employee, you'll normally start making student loan repayments from the April following the date you graduate or leave your course. HMRC will tell your employer how to work out and deduct the right amount.
- Once a year, HMRC tells the Student Loans Company what has been repaid. So, it is sensible to keep your payslips and P60 as a record of the repayments in case of any problems.
- Some employers put running totals of tax and deductions on your payslip. These are particularly useful for keeping track of your total student loan repayments.
- For more info, read our guide on Repaying student loans.
- Court orders and child maintenance
- A court can order deductions directly from your pay, for example for unpaid fines or for debt repayments to be handed to your creditors.
- The Child Support Agency (CSA) or Child Maintenance Service can also ask for a Deduction from Earnings Order (DEOs) for the maintenance of a child.

Tel: 01283 703043 Email: liza@heavenlyz.com

- If these orders are made for deductions, the employer can, if they choose to, take an additional £1 as an administration fee.
- This fee can only be charged if a deduction or partial deduction has been made.
- Employers often waive the fee but if they deduct it, it must be shown separately on the payslip with a description.
- Sick pay
- What is shown on your payslip will depend on how long you have been ill and your company's sick pay policy.
- Your employer is liable to pay you Statutory Sick Pay (SSP) if you're off work sick for four days or more in a row, and you meet certain conditions.
- SSP is treated like the wages or salary it replaces, so your employer will make deductions for tax, National Insurance and student loans, etc.
- Under your contract you might also be entitled to occupational sick pay.
- This will usually be shown as a separate figure – any SSP is likely to be deducted from occupational sick pay.
- Maternity, paternity and adoption pay
- If you're a mother who isn't at work because you've just had a baby and you're getting Statutory Maternity Pay (SMP), this will be shown on your payslip.
- You might also receive maternity pay, which will usually be shown separately.
- If parents choose to share time off, and take Shared Parental Leave (ShPL), they might be paid Shared Parental Pay (ShPP).
- If a child is adopted, Statutory Adoption Pay (SAP) will be paid to the new parent staying at home for a period after the adoption. If a couple jointly adopt, the other partner can be eligible for ASPP.
- Again, you must meet certain conditions to be able to qualify for these payments. They're all treated in the same way as ordinary earnings for tax and National Insurance.
- Workplace benefits
- If you get health insurance through your workplace or have a company car, these will be listed on your payslip and can affect your tax code.
- Repayment of season-ticket loans, cycle-to-work scheme loans and charitable donations (using the give-as-you-earn scheme) might also be shown.
- If you have signed up for one of these, then it should show up on your payslip.
- Find out more about Cars, insurance and other employee benefits.
- Other deductions - Any other deductions, like trade union subscriptions for example, should be shown.
- Summary of the year to date
- Your payslip might show how much you have been paid so far in this financial year (from 6 April to 5 April).
- It might also show totals for how much you have paid in tax, National Insurance, student loans and pensions.
- Net pay – what's left
- For many people, the most important figure on their payslip is net pay.
- So, what is net pay? It's the amount you get once all the deductions have been made. You should check this against your bank statement to make sure it matches what is paid in.
- Important messages - Some employers use a space on the pay slip for important messages. These might give you extra information about your pay or other information they want to share.

Tel: 01283 703043 Email: liza@heavenlyz.com

3.48 Regulatory Summary

Animal carers, whether personal or in business, are required by law to follow appropriate legislation summarised within this manual.

It would not be possible to include all legislation appropriate to animal care and legislation can be updated at any time. It is the responsibility of the animal carer, whether employer and employee, to ensure that relevant legislation is adhered to always.

Tel: 01283 703043 Email: liza@heavenlyz.com

4 Client/ Customer service

Client/ customer service is the provision of service to clients/ customers before, during and after a purchase (of products or services). It applies both to face to face and distance transactions. Success in client/ customer service is dependent on people (employers and employees) who are best able to relate to other people (customers).

Due to the repeat nature of the services/ products that this book typically covers, for the rest of this section we will refer to the customer as the "client" and to the employers/ employees within the business as the "supplier".

Suppliers who create strong and ongoing relationships with clients and who concentrate on clear, concise and appropriate language throughout client communication will be best placed for success.

Client/ customer service plays an important role in an organization's ability to generate income and revenue. From that perspective, customer service should be included as part of an overall approach to systematic improvement. One good or bad client customer service experience can change the entire perception a client/ customer holds towards the supplier. We will deal with client/ customer service in three broad areas: -

- Communicating with clients
- Recording information
- Dealing with conflicts

There are various forms of communication that support interaction between the supplier and the client, including the following: -

- Promotional material
- Supplier's Website
- Social media
- Email
- Telephone voice to voice
- Face to face
- Mobile phone messaging applications.
- Other electronic forms of communication (e.g. Skype)
- Posted letters

The typical animal care business relevant to this manual will follow this sequence in the supplier/ client relationship: -

1. Supplier has a business which operates only on word of mouth OR supplier has described services/ products attractive to a range of potential clients through various forms of advertising
2. A potential client recognises that their need may be served by the supplier through word of mouth OR through the supplier's adverts
3. The potential client contacts the supplier via means supported by the supplier and attractive to the client (e.g. the potential client turns up at the business premises/ the potential client phones or messages the supplier)
4. The supplier and the client agree services/ products to be provided (and, typically, the payment to be made by the client to the supplier)
5. The supplier provides the services/ products, the client has either paid upfront or pays at the end (either way is ok, but it is better that the order is made clear)
6. The services/ products supplied and the way that the supplier/ client relationship has been executed influences the future of the business. If the services/ products supplied were of a quality acceptable to the client and...: -
    a. ...the supplier/ client relationship has been executed **well**, the client may provide repeat business directly (i.e. they revisit the supplier) or, even better, the client may refer/ recommend the supplier to others (the power of positive referral/ recommendation should not be underestimated)

Tel: 01283 703043 Email: liza@heavenlyz.com

b. ...the supplier/ client relationship has been executed **poorly**, the client may: -

   i. do nothing
   ii. complain direct to the supplier (this is another form of supplier/ client interaction)
   iii. deter others from using the supplier, either via word of mouth or posting negative reviews on any form of media (note that the supplier may not know this is happening and that negative reviews about the business consistently outweigh the equivalent number of positive reviews)

Unfortunately, it is also worth noting that human nature is to be more vocal about things that go wrong and less vocal about things which are done well.

So, the key thing to note about providing good service to clients is that there are various points at which the client and the supplier communicate, and that at each of those points it is important to provide the best possible service.

So, how do we provide the best possible service? The answer lies in a set of behaviours that the supplier (being business owners or staff) should employ when dealing with the client at each touch point. These behaviours can include the following.

4.1 Client Service Behaviours

4.1.1 Professionalism

At all times, the supplier should act in a professional manner, even under provocation from an unreasonable client.

4.1.2 Clarity

At every touchpoint it is important to get as close to an agreed version of the truth as possible (absolute truth is very difficult to achieve). Help the client do this by being clear from the start, especially if you can predict the path that the client should follow to achieve their most beneficial outcome.

4.1.3 Patience

Listen to the customer – they may not be used to dealing with suppliers, so bear with them as they work through their communication and help you crystallise their comments.

4.1.4 Focus

We are all unique. What someone is saying to you is not necessarily what you understand.

Further, what we hear is not necessarily what we understand because our brains process what we receive, and our brain processing can deliver different outcomes dependant on many factors.

Therefore, the supplier sometimes must work hard to ensure that they clearly understand what the client is saying. Sometimes the client is clear, sometimes they are not. Sometimes the message is blatant, sometimes the supplier had to read between the lines. Most of the time, the client is honest and truthful, in few cases they are not (for whatever reason). The ability to properly listen and question is a skill that is highly beneficial.

4.1.5 Calmness

Do not let emotion overtake the conversation. This is very important, especially if the client is unhappy. Even if the client is highly emotional, do not reciprocate, avoid escalation, help the client manage their emotion, help navigate them to the facts.

HINT: don't become a robot 😉. Suppliers are people dealing with people – moderating emotion should leave the client understanding that the supplier is able to understand and is capable of reason and empathy.

4.1.6 Personality

This is somewhat linked to calmness, but it is more related to being engaging and motivating in the way we interact. Avoid monotone, vary the speed and pitch of your voice or your language ("appropriately", the client doesn't want to interact with an opera singer 😉) and find ways to engage with the client.

4.1.7 Brevity vs. Openness

There is a balance to be had between (i) encouraging clients to talk and provide details that they neither realise are relevant nor have they prepared to discuss AND (ii) keeping the dialogue limited such that we can

Tel: 01283 703043 Email: liza@heavenlyz.com

avoid items that are irrelevant or conversational dead-ends/ red herrings or conflating issues (i.e. things that which cause or increase confusion).

4.1.8 Efficiency

Do what you say you are going to do by the time you said you would do it. This is an aim sometimes difficult to achieve, but if you commit something to a client, then unless you subsequently agree a change with the client, the client will expect delivery. So, if things aren't going to plan, discuss this with the client, preferably before the plan comes undone.

4.1.9 Knowledge

Understand your subject matter and be ready and able to demonstrate it. If you are a supplier, you should understand the product or service being provided, how it's provided and what the impact will be on the client. Those impacts should be overall positive but if there are known negatives, be clear with the client upfront.

4.1.10 Positivity

Create a positive first impression, employ positive body language, including appropriate eye contact (some clients like eye contact/ some don't - HINT: don't "stare"/ blink naturally 😉).

If the supplier is upbeat, then this will influence the client and vice versa. No matter the conversation, no matter the media on which the conversation happens, a motivated, positive, friendly approach to dialogue will bring the greatest benefit to all parties.

People can range from wholly positive (rare) to wholly negative (also rare). When negativity is recognised, understand whether it is justified or not, and deal appropriately. Note thought that it is recommended that the supplier themselves always avoids any unnecessary negativity.

4.1.11 Recognition/ Acceptance

Where the client has brought you significantly positive benefits (e.g. they've referred more trade to you or they consistently give you good reviews), then it would be wise to consider rewarding that client appropriately.

Where the service provided has been sub-standard, then it is better to accept this as early as it is recognised and work with the client to provide an appropriate outcome for all.

4.1.12 External influences on the supplier

Work life and personal life should be independent of each other – i.e. neither should be negatively impacted by the other. However, we are all human, we are all fallible and we are all subject to the normal pressures of life. That said, it is up to the client whether they choose to be sympathetic if the supplier's service has been sub-standard due to something that has occurred in the supplier's private life.

4.1.13 Insightfulness regards the client

Try and understand the client as a person, ask yourself why they are being negative. If they are, try and understand any underlying concerns that are influencing their behaviour. They may have recently had an argument, a family tragedy, there are many things that change people's behaviour – if you as supplier can find the key to that change, then you are much better placed to help the client through their concerns.

4.1.14 Preparation

This assumes that you know the client is about to engage you. Normally, contact from clients is not random, it has a purpose. You may or may not have any idea what the client wants, but you should know the client and you should know your supplier/ client history. If not, remind yourself of that history, which you may keep in a computer application, a physical client card, an email.

Demonstrating your knowledge of the client/ supplier history may help put the client at ease/ may help reach a better outcome.

HINT: try to remember as many of your clients' names (even if it's just the pet's names 😉).

4.1.15 Outcome orientation

This assumes that you know the client is about to engage you and that you understand the purpose of the contact. Again, you should research the history, try to recognise the predicted best outcome of the contact and work towards that (without being inflexible).

Tel: 01283 703043 Email: liza@heavenlyz.com

4.1.16 Flexibility

Don't be rigidly tied to any predicted outcome, have a plan but do be flexible. Understand that clients have individual needs and that they may not completely fit your services/ products. Having a flexible approach helps reach best outcomes and can provide for opportunities that you hadn't previously recognised.

4.1.17 Persuasion

Assuming you have good knowledge, you understand the client and what you can and can't do to help, then you should be able to work through the problem with the client and be able to present reasonable arguments that the client is happy to support.

4.1.18 Tenacity

Essentially, don't give up on a client if they are unhappy. Persevere with them – the worst outcome is for a client to leave you because they are unhappy and yet, you don't understand why. This doesn't help you grow as a supplier.

4.1.19 Closure

Know when the discussion needs to end. If you have taken reasonable steps to support the client yet something is unresolvable, recognise when to close the dialogue. Don't leave the dialogue open ended, understand that the client may have potential next steps, accept that the client may take those further steps and be clear with the client that you feel the matter is closed.

4.1.20 Refinement

A client who raises a valid point, a piece of feedback which you hadn't previously considered, is providing you with a golden opportunity to provide better services/ products. Take criticism without offence.

4.2 Client Service in the salon

We can divide salon client service into the following main areas: -

4.2.1 Welcoming Clients

Greeting customers should be done in a friendly, positive, manner – no matter what previous experience the supplier has had with that client – with attention appropriately divided between the client(s) and, if present, their pet(s).

4.2.2 Appropriate communication with customers

At every point of supplier/ client contact, the supplier should be politely gathering information from the client. Experts in client service can elicit information from the client through natural conversation and without the client necessarily knowing that this is happening. Of course, the Data Protection Act should be considered when recording, retaining and discarding any of the following client information: -

- Dog's details
- Dog's owner and emergency contact details
- Dog's health status and current medication/ treatments
- Dog's behaviour with dogs/ people (especially if at another salon)
- Dog's previous grooming history
- Client's expectations of the service or products to be provided
- Client's requirements for each individual dog, taking into consideration pet trims, trims for ease of management and traditional breed standard show styles
- Client's awareness of cost, happiness to accept quote (and any potential variances) and duration of groom/ potential pick up time

4.2.3 Care, management, safety and security of clients in the workplace

It is best that client's movement around the workplace are restricted to a safe area. There will be areas where the client may need to go (e.g. to sign) and there may be areas where the client does not need to go (e.g. where staff valuables are stored whilst working).

Tel: 01283 703043 Email: liza@heavenlyz.com

Even though you may consider your workplace safe, staff are normally well trained in the assessment of risks in the workplace, clients not so – therefore clients may be less aware of certain dangers, restricted client movement is recommended.

If a client must move into an area normally authorised only for staff, ensure that they are carefully escorted by a member of staff always.

Each client should be treated with at least a minimum acceptable standard of care. They should be responsible for their own belongings whilst in the workplace, suppliers should consider a clearly observable disclaimer regards liability for lost or damaged client belongings (this would extend to any parking facilities on the supplier's premises).

Have a policy for the rare occasion where clients may become ill whilst at your workplace.

4.2.4 Client exit from the workplace

There are various activities to carry out when exiting the client from the workplace: -

- Ensure that the client has paid in full
- Ensure that the client has had opportunity to make another booking
- Ensure that the client (or the client's representative) is happy with the outcome and is aware, understands and has had the opportunity to discuss any deviation from requirement
- Client (or representative) to confirm/ approve the outcome in writing and that the animal has been returned without presenting illness or injury (n.b. consider the scenario where the client's representative collects the dog and either mistreats the dog before presenting to client or does not present the dog to the client in the same state as the dog left the supplier).
- Ensure that the client is cared for, safe and secure until off the premises

4.3 Managing Conflict

There is always potential for conflict in any relationship.

The best way to manage conflict is to avoid it in the first place. There are many ways to do this, including considering the behaviours previously mentioned, ensure that as far as possible the supplier discloses to the client everything that they need to know (i.e. be upfront), consider the typical conflict scenarios that may arise and prepare an approach for each (rehearse/ role play if necessary).

As already stated, conflict – especially conflict not resolved to the satisfaction of the client, can have impacts on the supplier's business.

Here, we consider several scenarios that may typically arise in the dog grooming salon, complete with suggestions regards potential routes to mitigate this conflict.

4.3.1 Payment disputes

Be clear upfront regards the likely price, whether the price being provided is a fixed quote or a more flexible estimate and ensure the client clearly understands the typical problems that may cause the price (or the service given for that price) to change.

Consider that having done this, a dispute is still raised at the point that the client returns to collect the dog. Discuss the client's concerns and, if reasonable, modify your position. If not reasonable, consider whether you wish to have repeat/ referred business from the client and consider whether you have a defendable position if the client decides to raise negative publicity (via any media, especially now on social media) against the supplier's business.

At which point, decide how to deal. If you still expect to charge the client a price that they disagree with, explain to the client politely but firmly that the dog can only be returned once the correct amount is paid. If alternately, you decide to cut your losses, inform the client of your plan explaining why you think it is unfair and that you may make other similar establishments in the area aware of the client's actions.

If the money owed is small, letting the client go without payment and not allowing them back may, in the longer term, be a better option (and there is significant precedence for this approach).

Note that it is rarely worthwhile to invest time and money in a legal route to regain the relatively small amount that the client is likely to owe you – it is better to invest this time and money upfront to ensure that your service is of the highest standards.

Tel: 01283 703043 Email: liza@heavenlyz.com

4.3.2 Invalid card/currency

There are various legitimate reasons why the client's card/ currency ("tender") may be invalid. Card's expire, so do notes and coins (though less frequently). There are also other, less legitimate, reasons why client's tender may be declined, and the supplier needs to be prepared for these instances.

Have a procedure in place to deal with these kinds of instances. Understand your rights as a supplier when confronted with a customer refusing to pay for services. Consider whether you wish to charge clients upfront either the full expected fee or a proportion of it – this may not avoid commercial disputes, but it will provide clarity to the customer if the dispute arises.

Even if not apparent at the time of collection most clients will have access to alternative forms of payment, even if the supplier may have to wait (the supplier will have to balance the risk of non-payment if the animal is returned to the client and the payment can be deferred).

4.3.3 Accidental injury to dog

When working in an animal care environment, accidental injury to animals is a potential, but obviously highly unwelcome, occurrence. As always, it is better to prevent/ mitigate this type of occurrence but where an injury occurs, the following is recommended as a basic procedure to follow: -

- Alert all other staff where you can simultaneously keep the animal safe/ treat the animal
- Check vital signs/ consider use of CPCR whilst calling the vet for telephone support
- Dependant on severity of injury, consider: -
    - Informing owner and arrange to meet at vets
    - Securing all other dogs
    - Stopping salon activities
    - Closing salon
    - Preventing public access
    - Contact vet for advice, follow vet advice
    - If required after consultation with vet: -
        - Have vet visit premises or transfer animal to vet
        - Within 12-24 hours Inform your business insurance and any other appropriate party (e.g. management)
- Record the incident and file
- Review, identify root cause, confirm that appropriate controls remain in place and consider refining procedures

4.3.4 Time management

This essentially refers to ensuring that the supplier, the client and all others involved in the care for a specific animal are all aware of planned timings. For example, the business is open from 9am until 5pm, the dog is due to start a 2-hour appointment at 3pm but does not arrive until 4pm. This means that the appointment would, if carried out, end at 6pm having a potentially negative impact on the business (business consents may restrict times of operation), staff (staff are required to be paid for work done and are potentially due overtime, they may also have appointments from 5pm onwards), the client (the client may not be aware of the need for 2 hours).

To prevent this kind of occurrence, use a flexible, backed up, appointment system (whether paper or electronic, generic calendar or appointment system specific to the industry), be clear up front with your clients, write their appointments down, publish them in some way that is private between you and the client (e.g. any commonly available appointment booking service), consider the use of reminders to the client (e.g. text/ email/ social media). For clients with special needs, consider setting a rigid recurring appointment system (i.e. appointments that recur at the same time/ days/ dates).

4.3.5 Dispute over outcome vs. requirements

On arrival to collect their animal, the client indicates that the outcome is not as they required. Ways to reduce disputes such as this: -

- Retain record cards per animal, maintain grooming notes.
- At point of animal drop-off, record the client's requirements and assess the dog for health and grooming. Discuss any impacts that the dog's health and coat may have on the client's requirements *with* the client. Agree an acceptable outcome (acceptable to both – groomers should not capitulate to a client where there is a clear health imperative for the dog) and record it. Require the client to confirm their agreement by signature.
- Also, get the client to confirm that whilst the dog is in the groomer's care, it is the responsibility of the groomer to decide if, mid-groom, there is a clear reason to modify the requirements. That is, there may be something that you are unaware of when the client drops the animal off, but then becomes apparent during the groom and in a situation where you may not be able to contact the client.
- Carry out the grooming procedure according to the requirements. Where there is a clear need to deviate from the requirements, attempt to contact and discuss with the client. If you can contact the client, agree on the appropriate course of action. If you cannot contact the client, the onus is on the groomer (potentially with management support) to achieve the best outcome for the dog. If you deviate from the requirements, have a clear reason for doing so and record this reason.
- At the point of animal collection, explain the grooming process, any deviation from requirements and the attempts you made to contact the client. If the client is still unhappy, record their concerns and escalate to management.

4.3.6 Animal welfare issues

Animal welfare is paramount in our profession. Caring for a living being is above all other concerns. As professionals, we pride ourselves in implementing the best animal care possible.

That said, all living beings caring for other living beings make mistakes. Though we put in place appropriate procedures, training and knowledge, mistakes do occur.

For any mistake, refer to section 4.3.3 paying attention to the requirement to "Review and refine procedures".

For anything else, there is no excuse – as professional animal carers we are required to ensure that we have taken all possible steps to ensure that we are fully equipped to provide the best service and the safest/ most beneficial environment for the animals in our care.

Tel: 01283 703043 Email: liza@heavenlyz.com

5 Workplace Health and Safety

Health and Safety legislation is sometimes over looked. If you follow the checklist below you should be able to easily understand what's required in your work place.

It is advisable to regularly review health and safety with fresh eyes to put in place UK law requirements. More importantly, regular health and safety reviews increase protection to yourself and other life.

Heavenlyz operates a workplace Health and Safety consultancy service where an experienced Health and Safety qualified person conducts a workplace visit, makes an assessment and provides a written health and safety audit that will help you put in place relevant legislation such as RISK/COSHH.

Heavenlyz can also provide written, individual, operational manuals that will satisfy local authorities and will include animal care consent forms, fire escape routes, staff inductions and manual handling.

The following are recommended codes of practice to follow/ information or equipment required to be available/ displayed in an animal care workplace: -

- Health and safety policy or poster (applicable where there are 5 or more employees)
- Risk Assessment (an ongoing process)
- COSHH Assessment (an ongoing process)
- Product Data Sheets
- Fire Risk Assessment – policy and escape routes
- Wall mounted fire extinguishers, serviced annually with signage
- Personal Protective Equipment (PPE) provided and full training of how to use given and recorded
- Portable Appliance Testing (PAT) recommended annually for daily used electrical items outside manufacturer's guarantee.
- First Aid Kit for Humans and Animals
- Appointed First Aider – a display of who is on duty
- Accident book stored in a locked facility
- Employment Legislation and Insurance policy
- Disability and Equality policy
- Waste Transfer Notes
- Staff Induction (ongoing)
- Staff Training Record (ongoing)
- Client records, stored in a locked facility
- Accounts
- Emergency procedures specific to location or situation

The key thing is to ensure that you are operating safely and legally. Heavenlyz can help you achieve this quickly, providing full consultation, including implement of all Health and Safety legislation needs where required.

5.1 Workplace Design

The following design factors will influence how your workplace ultimately looks and operates: -

- Accessibility – for members of the public including adequate safe place to load and unload dogs coming and going from the salon. It's advisable to contact your local authority to discuss highway access/ exit in detail to ensure the salon is operating within the local authority conditions.
- Wellbeing – the correct bath/ work bench/ table heights should be employed.

Tel: 01283 703043 Email: liza@heavenlyz.com

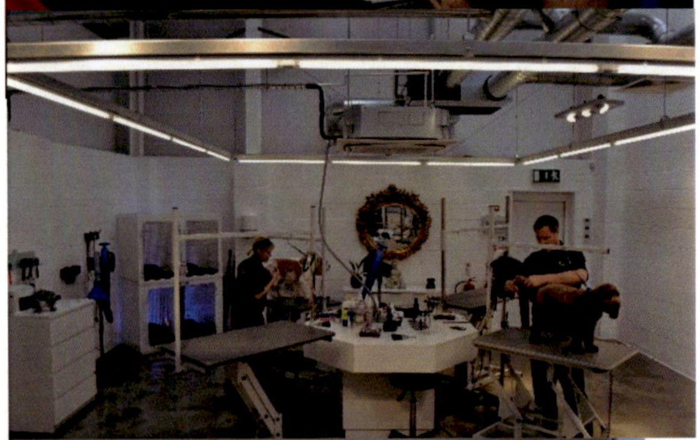

- Efficiency – Lights and windows should be designed into appropriate places to shed enough light onto the dog being groomed (especially when grooming darker coats). The correct number of electrical sockets and adequate drainage will all contribute to harmony within the salon. It is especially useful to consider the use of both light and dark backgrounds to contrast with, respectively, darker and lighter coloured coats.
- Adequate space and facilities – if room allows, include separate bathing and drying areas. This does not necessarily mean separate rooms but far enough from each other to avoid styling a dog on potentially wet floors.

Install housing in form of collapsible cages or a bank of cages or a blanket on the floor associated with a hook on a wall attached to a sufficient length of lead (to allow the dog to both stand up and sit down in comfort) and secure collar. Ensure that dog housing is always easily observable. Provide adequate storage for towels, detergents and personal belongings. Provide catering facilities for employees (and perhaps customers).

Health and safety considerations – the workplace should be designed to meet with current health and safety and fire regulations (e.g. steps and paths to the premises must be safe). Toilet facilities must be provided for staff (and perhaps customers) and these must be kept in a clean, hygienic, condition. A main supply circuit breaker (isolator) must be provided and all electrical sockets must be safely installed.

5.1.1 Risk Warning Signs

Our workplaces contain significant hazards. Design should include provision for appropriate signage. All substances and areas of concern should display a warning sign to alert of possible risks as follows: -

Tel: 01283 703043 Email: liza@heavenlyz.com

5.1.2 Minimising Environmental Damage

Day to day operations and activities within the animal care workplace can have an impact on the environment. Consider an action plan to help minimise your salons impact on the environment and reduce your carbon footprint, suggestions as follows;

- Use energy (i.e. electricity) in a responsible and economic way to minimise negative impact on the environment. This can be achieved, for example, by turning off lights as you leave a room; after bathing and blasting, remove as much water as possible to reduce dog coat drying time prior to cabinet/ blast drying.
- Use water in a responsible and economic way to minimise negative impact on the environment. This can be achieved by using a hydro-bath that reuses water, avoiding excessive use of shampoo or conditioner (which would lead to wasting water when rinsing/ removing from coat).
- Use substances and materials that are not environmentally damaging or harmful to humans/ animals.
- Minimise waste, choosing to recycle or re-use wherever possible and minimising waste to landfills
- Prevent damage to the environment resulting from release of polluting substances
- When travelling, plan to minimise environmental impact of excessive mileage. Perhaps operate a collection and delivery service, operate in specific areas on different days, collecting and returning more than one dog at a time.
- Identify specific tasks that consume resources and continually review to ensure best practice and most efficient procedures followed.

5.2 Animal Care Workplace Construction

As with all animal care industry specific businesses, the most important consideration is the protection of life (welfare of humans or animals in our care). For animals in our care, we use the 5 animal needs, which vary in detail from publication to publication, but generally adhere to the following: -

- Security
- Protection from injury and disease
- Protection from mental suffering (fear and stress)
- Opportunity to express natural and normal for that individual dog behaviour
- Opportunity to defecate and urinate

Animals are generally more relaxed when they feel comfortable and secure. So, it is worth planning to create a relaxed atmosphere purposely designed for the animals that will attend your premises and for who you will temporarily care.

5.2.1 Construction materials

All construction materials must be able to withstand constant use, be easy to clean and provide the ability to easily remove hair from walls and floors. All floor surfaces must be designed to be non-slip, must be good at absorbing sound and must be light reflective.

Tel: 01283 703043 Email: liza@heavenlyz.com

5.2.2 Holding Units

The security and safety of the dogs in our care is paramount. Systems to prevent accidental escape must be considered. Many salons operate a double or triple door system. This can be as basic as a half stable door placed between the grooming area and main reception exit door.

All cages should be easily to clean, have no rough edges that may cause injuries and have a secure locking mechanism.

Cages comes in many forms and it will depend on the initial budget and space.

Enrichments are a way of enhancing the experience of the animals in your care. Enrichments are as simple as the provision of fresh water, adequate opportunities to go to the toilet and time enough for personal contact.

The holding unit or temporary housing should have a suitable surface to provide comfort. The following surfaces are common: -

- towel – the fabric provides comfort and padding but is difficult to launder
- dry bulky rubber mat – easy to clean or sterilise, but padding is lacking, and it looks unappealing to the owner
- vet bed – looks professional and appealing, retains warmth, provides adequate padding and launders and dries easily. It is expensive to buy initially but will last years if not chewed.

The temperature in the holding unit must not fall below 7 degrees centigrade. Additional warmth may need to be provided. However, many of the dogs visiting the salon are housed in centrally heated homes so Heavenlyz recommends that the environment is (a) initially maintained at a constant room temp of 18 – 22 degrees centigrade and (b) environmental temperatures – and animals' reactions to those temperatures – are monitored such that appropriate adjustments can be made.

Tel: 01283 703043 Email: liza@heavenlyz.com

6 Equipment Management

Heavenlyz recommends that a log of bought equipment is maintained, including the date that the equipment was bought, the dates by which it runs out of warranty and the date by which it must be next tested (e.g. "PAT"). A log of this type is known as an asset register.

Remember always to check that the equipment you require is to hand and that the area to be used for grooming is safe and secure. If the equipment is found to be damaged: -

- **Do not use it** (as it could damage the dog)
- Inform supervisor/ other salon employees/ attendees
- Label damaged equipment, to alert others not to use it.
- If applicable, dispose of it in an appropriate manner
- If applicable, repair or replace equipment

6.1 Clippers

An exploded Clipper Blade Mechanism is shown in the picture to the right. A clipper blade is a reasonably complex item of engineering, can be significantly costly to the owner and is therefore worthy of a good level of care and security.

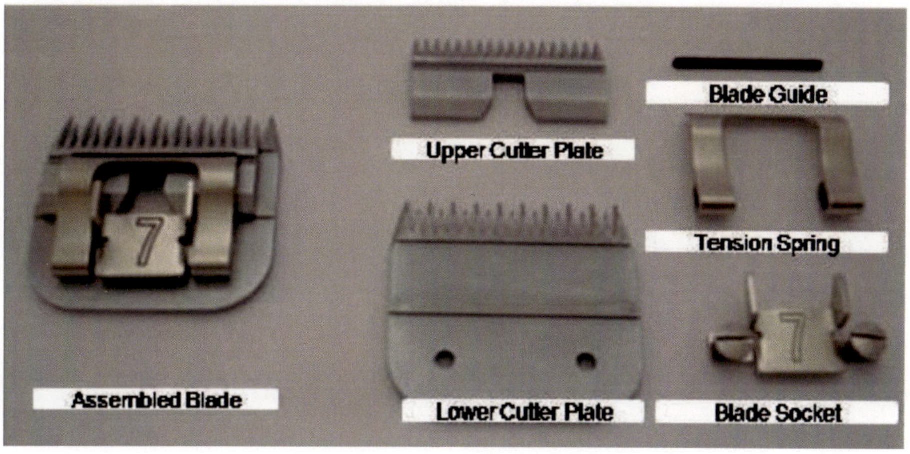

6.2 Scissors

The constituent parts of a pair of scissors are shown in the picture below. Scissors can also be significantly costly to the owner and are also therefore worthy of a good level of care and security.

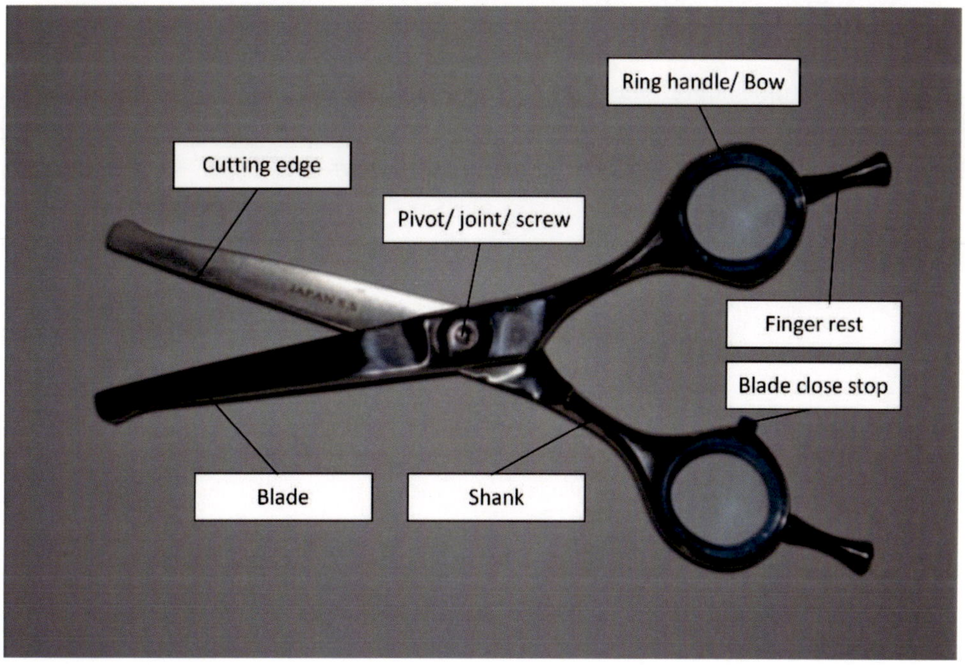

Tel: 01283 703043 Email: liza@heavenlyz.com

7 Cleanliness of the Work Environment

All areas of the work environment should be cleaned regularly to prevent the spread of disease and create a professional image for the clients.

Draw up a default cleaning rota to list what should be cleaned on an as-soon-as-it's-used, daily, weekly or monthly basis, stating who is responsible for that duty. Enforce the rota appropriately.

There are many suitable disinfectants available, properties for the ideal disinfectant follow: -

- Economical to use
- Pleasant smelling, not too overpowering to animals (remember that (a) an animals sense of smell is more acute than our own, in some instances – e.g. dogs – **much** more acute than human and that (b) animals and humans may find different smells attractive – i.e. a smell that a human likes may not be a smell that an animal likes)
- Effective against a wide range of diseases
- Easy to dilute
- Non-toxic to animals and humans (e.g. Phenols should not be used around cats)
- Non-staining
- Readily available
- Good shelf life
- Manufacturers usage guidelines available (these must be followed)

Disinfectant effectiveness varies, mainly due to: -

- Over dilution (which lessens the effect of the product)
- Under dilution (which can lead to a toxic and potentially corrosive substance)
- Temperature of water used to dilute – some disinfectants are more effective in hot water
- Contact time - disinfectants need to be in contact for a specific length of time to be effective

The use of disinfectant must be associated with: -

- The provision and wearing of appropriate PPE
- Training/ instruction for all staff on safe use of the chosen disinfectant

Never mix disinfectants – this could inadvertently create a toxic substance, that will be dangerous to both humans and animals, whether by direct contact or vapour inhalation.

Tel: 01283 703043 Email: liza@heavenlyz.com

8 Sterilisation and cleaning of equipment

All grooming equipment used should be thoroughly cleaned between dogs and, in addition, sterilised where indicated by a manufacturer's schedule.

The following table summarises the cleaning and maintenance of various types of equipment commonly found in the grooming salon.

Equipment	Cleaning/Sterilising	Maintenance/ storage
Nylon/ Bristle Brush	Remove hair/ wash, disinfect UV sterilise	Replace worn broken bristles
Slicker, pin brushes	Remove hair/ UV sterilise	Replace damaged teeth
Clippers	Remove hair/oil movable parts	Check cord and annual PAT/ service test
Clipper Blades	Remove hair/ oil whilst running/ UV sterilise	Oil keep out damp environment/ replace when worn/ sharpen as needed
Combs	Remove hair/ wash / disinfect/ UV sterilise	Replace when worn/ keep out damp environment prevent rusting
Coat king, stripping knifes, matt breakers	Remove hair/ UV sterilise	Replace when worn/ store damp free environment
Dryer/ blaster	Remove hair from filters/ wheels	Check cord regularly/ annual PAT and service
muzzles	Wash, disinfect and dry	Replace if worn
Scissors/thinners	Remove hair and sterilise/ oil blade and pivot/ UV sterilise	Oil pivot joint/ blade. Replace if damaged/ sharpen as required. Keep in padded case. Do not use on anything but clean dry hair, as expensive and will destroy cutting surface. Store in a damp free environment
Restraint straps/ loops	Wash, disinfect and dry	Replace if worn
Towels	Remove hair/ wash and dry	Keep out damp environment stacked neatly ready for use

8.1 Cleaning

Using the proper method to clean equipment prior to sterilisation is key to the sterilisation process. Cleaning is the removal of foreign material (e.g. hair, faecal matter, mucous, urine) from grooming equipment and is normally accomplished using water and a suitable detergent.

Thorough cleaning is required before high-level disinfection and/or sterilisation because inorganic/ organic materials that remain on equipment surfaces can dry or "bake on" to the equipment (making their subsequent removal much more difficult and will interfere with the effectiveness of the equipment sterilisation or disinfection processes

Tel: 01283 703043 Email: liza@heavenlyz.com

Also, if soiled, the removal process becomes more difficult and the disinfection or sterilisation process becomes less effective or ineffective. Badly soiled equipment (e.g. via diarrhoea) should be pre-soaked or rinsed to prevent any solids drying as well as to soften or remove prior to being cleaned. Once all debris/ dirt is removed from equipment, sterilisation may begin.

8.2 Sterilisation methods

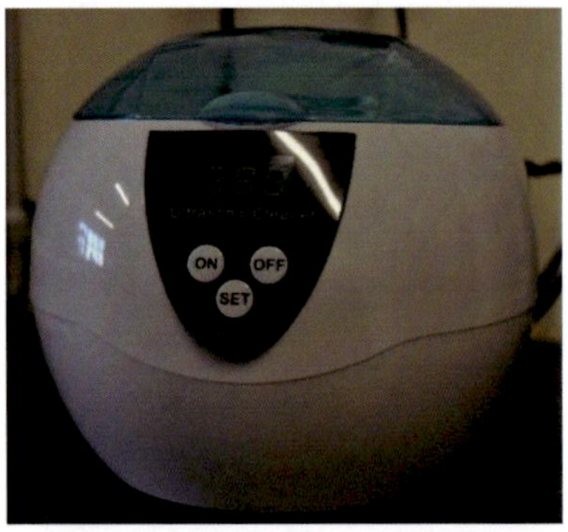

There are several know sterilisation methods used, the most common being described in the following sections.

8.2.1 Ultrasonic Sterilisation

Ultrasonic sterilisation is a process that uses high frequency sound and an appropriate cleaning solvent (sometimes ordinary tap water) to clean items.

Ultrasonic cleaners are used to clean many different types of objects, including combs and blades but the use of water and detergent has its limitations as, if not properly dried following use, this may cause equipment to rust.

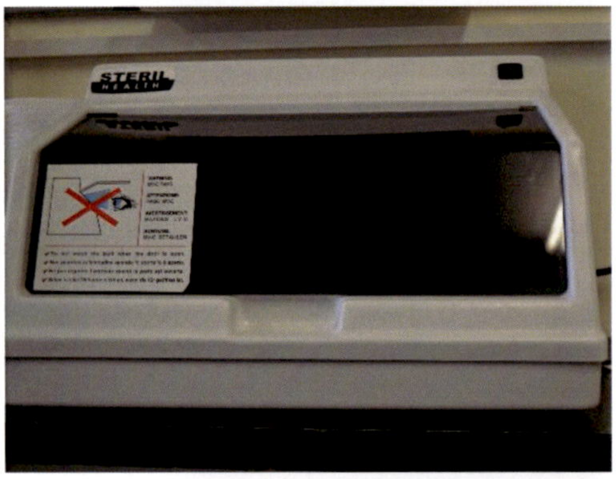

8.2.2 Ultraviolet Sterilisation

Ultraviolet (UV) cabinets offer quick and convenient sterilisation of all equipment. As this method uses no heat or chemicals, it is potentially the most enduring solution.

In some UV machines the equipment being sterilised must be turned over or rotated, to ensure that all sides of the equipment are equally sterilised.

UV sterilisation kills all known types of micro-organisms and bacteria. Requires no toxic chemicals or cleaning additives. Equipment remains cool, dry and ready for use.

8.2.3 Barbicide

Barbicide is a cold chemical form of sterilisation which requires the correct amount of barbicide mixed with water as per manufacturer's instructions, the efficiency of the solution will be reduces and will require frequent changes, which can be daily dependence of amount used and manufacturer's recommendation.

This form of solution is only appropriate for low risk items, those that have not contacted a known parasite, fungal or infection. Even then, the item must be thoroughly cleaned prior to being submerged totally in the fluid for the recommended contact time.

Items suitable to be classed as low risk infection are combs, brushes, blades and comb attachments.

8.2.4 Clippercide®

Clippercide ® is a 5-in-1 chemical spray sterilisation. Clippercide ® Spray disinfects and lubricates, as well as cools, cleans, and prevents rust on clippers. Regular use will reduce friction and prolong clipper life. The aerosol spray blasts away hairs, and helps cool blades. Clippercide® claims that its formula kills fungi, TB, bacteria, and HIV.

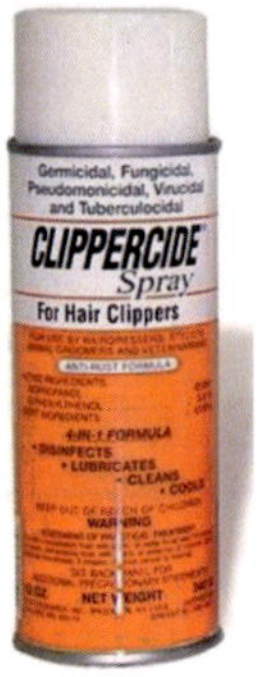

Tel: 01283 703043 Email: liza@heavenlyz.com

9 Breed Classification

First, let's set a few general principles.

9.1 Reasons for dogs

Dogs are kept for a variety of reasons around the world to include: -

- Companionship
- **Working for humans** of which there are numerous categories including: - Guard Dogs; Herding; Search and rescue; Tracking Dogs; Police Dogs; Detection Dogs.
- Draught and Sledge
- **Assistance Dogs** guide dogs/ hearing dogs
- **Support Dogs** improve quality of peoples' lives, primarily those who have physical disabilities or who suffer from life impacting conditions (e.g. epilepsy/ autism)
- **Therapy and emotional support dogs** provide services such as seizure alert and cancer detection
- Breeding and Showing

9.2 Reasons for Grooming

Let's ask one of the most fundamental questions, "Why do we groom animals?" Well, here are some reasons, you may be able to think of others.

- Prevents the coat from matting
- Keeps coat in good condition
- Aids Health Checking
- Reduces skin complaints
- Reduces Odour
- Helps with bonding
- Maintains a healthy coat
- Looks nice
- Supports specific lifestyles

9.3 Breed Categorisation

Dogs can be categorised as one of the following: -

- **Pure breed/ pedigrees** – both parents are the same kennel club registered breed
- **Cross breed** – a cross between two pedigrees
- **Mongrels** – a mix of three or more breeds

Regards pure breeds/ pedigrees, we'll use the example of the UK Kennel Club. There are many breeds of dog eligible for Kennel Club registration and these can be categorised into seven main groups: -

- **Hounds** use either sight or scent for hunting purposes and therefore may be very independent.
- **Gundogs** are bred to work in the field or water, to hunt, point and retrieve.
- **Terriers** are ratters and vermin hunters, very keen and wilful.
- **Utility** is a mixed group of dogs each with their own characters or working abilities.
- **Working group** includes guarding and defence dogs.
- **Pastoral** are the shepherding and herding breeds used to keep flocks and herds under control.
- **Toys** are companion dogs.

Tel: 01283 703043 Email: liza@heavenlyz.com

9.3.1 Hounds

Sight Hounds are racers such as the Whippet, Saluki, Afghan or Greyhound. These dogs are bred for short, intense bursts of exercise followed by long rests. They make for very lazy companions, extremely happy to remain docile providing they are provided with short opportunities to expend energy and to keep their well-toned muscles in peak condition.

Scent Hounds are built for a day's endurance, lasting all day if needed. Breeds include Beagle, Basset, Dachshund and Fox Hound. These breeds prefer long off the lead walks through areas providing lots of different scents to stimulate their mind and explore. These dogs are intelligent.

9.3.2 Gundogs

Bred to work in the field and water, e.g. Labrador Retriever, Cocker, Field Spaniel. Happy to be mentally and physically challenged daily, although the intensity of exercise will depend on the individual breed. It is recommended to research the breed origin and purpose to ensure that exercise requirements are met.

9.3.3 Terriers

For example, Airedale Terrier, Cairn and Scottish Terriers. Both the short legged and long-legged terrier require a high level of exercise to remain healthy. Originally bred to hunt for small rodents, they have a determined intense character and a high level of intelligence. They require mental stimulation as well as physical activity.

9.3.4 Utility

A mixed group of different characters and abilities, for example Lhasa Apso, Chow Chow and Poodle. Study the breed to understand the exercise requirements taking into consideration the origin and breed purpose.

9.3.5 Working group

The working group dogs are bred specifically for guarding and defending (e.g. Boxer, Great Dane and Doberman). A diverse group of dogs, with a variety of size, weight, body shape and purpose. In general, the working group will require a high level of mental stimulation alongside moderate exercise to maintain their health. Working breeds are highly intelligent and easier to train

9.3.6 Pastoral

Shepherding, guarding stock and herding dogs, such as the Old English sheepdog, German Shepherd Dog and Border collie. Bred to maintain a moderate level of activity all through the day. Extremely intelligent and require mental stimulation as well as a high level of physical activity, including playing several games of fetch in addition to long off the lead walks daily. This breed will excel at agility, fly ball and herding trails.

9.3.7 Toys

Toy breeds are generally bred to be companions and generally require less exercise than other breeds. Due to their small size they may tire easily.

Tel: 01283 703043 Email: liza@heavenlyz.com

10 Basic Anatomy and physiology

During your studies you will hear and see words used to describe an area of the dog. Some terms will be more commonly used than others. Familiarising yourself with basic anatomy will help you to understand what is required when grooming. Knowledge of anatomy will help with many aspects of your work. This section includes diagrams and narrative summarising the basic anatomical terms that the qualification requires.

1. Belly
2. Cheek
3. Chest
4. Chin
5. Crest of Neck
6. Croup
7. Ear
8. Elbow
9. Eye
10. Flank
11. Flew
12. Hip Joint
13. Hock
14. Loin
15. Metacarpus (consisting four long bones with five digits in foreleg of the dog, digit 1 being dew claw)
16. Metatarsal (hind leg dew claw, often absent)
17. Muzzle
18. Nostrils
19. Occiput (flat area at back of the skull)
20. Pad (underside of the Paw)
21. Pastern
22. Paw
23. Perineal area (area between anus and genitals)
24. Point of the Shoulder
25. Rear Stopper Pads
26. Ribs
27. Rump
28. Spine
29. Sternum
30. Stifle
31. Stop
32. Tail
33. Throat Latch
34. Tongue Median Groove
35. Topline (not shown – an imaginary line from the withers to the tail set)
36. Tuck up
37. Umbilicus
38. Withers

10.1 General anatomical notes

This section is designed to help enhance safety and wellbeing of dogs in your care.

The following should be noted and employed to make the grooming process more enjoyable for all involved: -

- A dog's joint should never be over flexed. Feet/ limbs should never be raised higher than the joint to which they're attached, as doing so risks causing pain/ injury.
- The body weight of the dog must be supported always, especially with long backed breeds, long legged breeds or aged dogs.
- A non-slip surface should always be used to make the dog feel secure and prevent accidental strains through slipping

10.2 Skull

Different breeds have very different head shapes which are generally categorised into: -

- **Dolichocephalic** – long & thin (e.g. Greyhound)
- **Mesocephalic** – "normal" head shape (e.g. Labrador)
- **Brachiocephalic** – short and broad (e.g. Pug)

Even though all three skull shapes differ they contain the same major bone structure, consisting of: -

- **Cranium** – the structure that encloses the brain
- **Occiput -** posterior (back/ raised) portion of the head or skull

Tel: 01283 703043 Email: liza@heavenlyz.com

- **Maxilla** – the upper part of the jaw
- **Mandible** – the lower part of the jaw

10.3 Teeth

Dogs have teeth that are positioned at different intervals of the jaw. The teeth have evolved to perform different purposes and are divided into four groups: -

- **Canines** – long and sharp for catching and holding prey
- **Incisors** – help hold prey in position
- **Premolars** – allows the shearing of chunks of meat off a carcass bone to prepare for swallowing
- **Molars** – perform a shearing and tearing action.

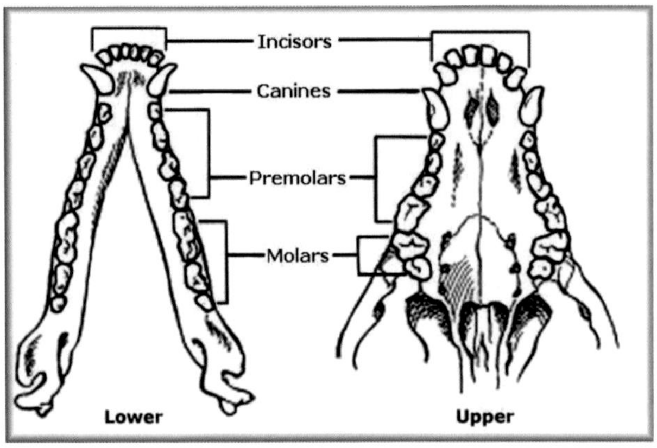

The teeth are arranged as per the picture, in the Mandible (Lower part of the jaw) and the Maxilla (Upper part of the jaw).

10.4 Coat Types

For the purposes of the qualification, coat types can be summarised as follows: -

- **Hairless** either having little or no hair at all (e.g. American Hairless Terrier)
- **Short/smooth coats** are short and tight to the body are low maintenance and only requiring the removal of dead coat to give a glossy finish (e.g. Boxers, Dobermans, and Staffordshire Bull Terriers).
- **Double Coats** consist of a dense soft undercoat concealed by a longer topcoat and are normally one of two types: -
    - **Type one** –require a lot of grooming to remove dead undercoat with little or no trimming. These coats can be tidied but essentially remain untrimmed (e.g. Rough Collie, German Shepherd Dog, Samoyed and St Bernard).
    - **Type two** – trimmed (e.g. Lhasa Apso, Shih Tzu, Old English Sheepdog).

The following breeds have a much longer top coat. For practical pet trims their coats should be shortened in a style appropriate for the breed and the dog's lifestyle: -

- **Corded Coat** – a coat of dreadlocks (e.g. Hungarian Puli, Komondor).
- **Wool Coats** – these coats do not shed hair ("moult"). However, they require more maintenance than other coats, specific blow-drying techniques and trimming styles (e.g. Bichon, Poodle).
- **Silk Coats** – The most important feature of a silk coat is texture, not length (E.g. Afghan Hound, Yorkshire terrier, Lhasa Apso (when in full coat) and Spaniels such as Cavalier King Charles Spaniel).
- **Wire Coats** are harsh, with a dense topcoat and soft undercoat. To maintain the correct texture, a wire coat should only be hand stripped. If a wire coat is clipped it may damage the coat texture and/ or density, making future hand strips difficult. Breed examples that have a wire coat include Border Terrier, Wire Fox Terrier, West Highland White Terrier.

10.5 Coat Colour and Patterns

Coats are varied in length and textures and come in a stunning variety of colours. There are also many different coat patterns (e.g. bi-colour, tri-colour, brindles, spots, merles, harlequins). It is not necessary to manage coat patterns, however, getting the shampoo, conditioner and supplements right will help bring out the best in the dog's coat.

There are a variety of commercially available shampoos which claim to enhance the natural coat colour of a dog's coat. For example, "white dog shampoos" claim to make white dogs sparkle and "black dog shampoos" claim to make black dogs coat black and glossy. Generally, a white shampoo could be used on a dark coat, but a dark shampoo should not be used on a white coat.

Tel: 01283 703043 Email: liza@heavenlyz.com

Caution coats on some breeds of dog may change texture, colour and density once clipped. Neutering of a dog by either castration or spaying as well as certain medication and ailments may also have significant changes on the dog's coat.

Tel: 01283 703043 Email: liza@heavenlyz.com

11 Dog Skin and Hair

A dog's coat is made up of hairs, requiring the groomer to have a basic knowledge of skin and hair structure and hair cycles.

11.1 Skin Function

The main functions of the skin follow: -

- to insulate
- maintain and regulate body temperature
- maintains hydration
- acts as a barrier from harmful foreign substances
- enables sensation.

Damaged skin will try to heal by forming scar tissue. The skin sheds through a continuous hardening process called keratinization and this can be commonly seen on bony prominences such as elbows and noses of geriatric dogs (where hair is sparse, and the area is exposed). This is considered acceptable and healthy in dogs.

11.2 Skin Structure

The skin is made up of three protective layers as follows: -

- Epidermis
- Dermis
- Subcutaneous Layer

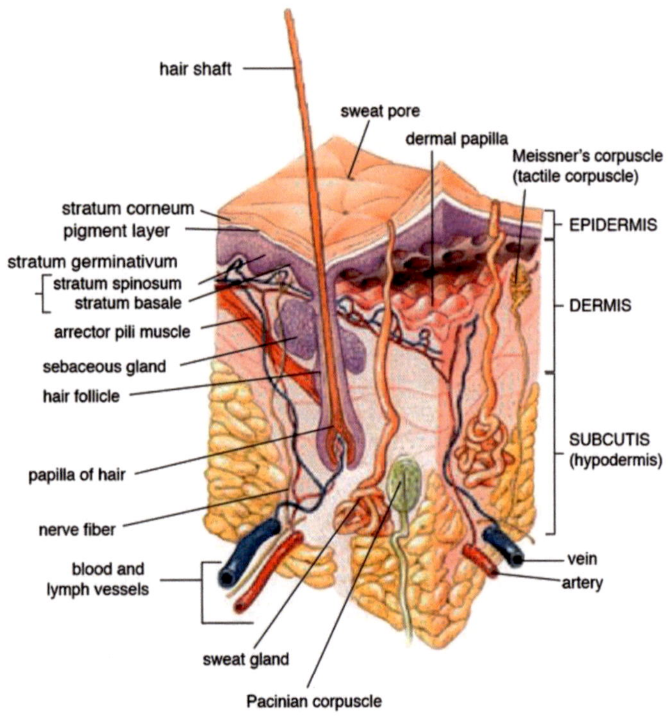

11.2.1 Epidermis

Being the layer in contact with the outside world, the epidermis is the body's environmental shield. It is made up of tough keratinized cells that are continuously formed, live and then shed away from the surface. In some dogs and in some areas of the body, epidermis contains dark brown pigment that screens the body from harmful sunrays rays.

11.2.2 Dermis

The dermis is the second layer composed of a network of connective tissue that also contains nerves, blood vessels, hair follicles, and sweat and oil glands.

The dermis supports and nourishes the epidermis. The blood vessels that supply the epidermis with nutrients are in the dermis. Blood vessels also regulate skin and body temperature. Sensory nerves and hair follicles are also in the dermis. The skin responds to the sensations of touch, pain, itch, heat, and cold etc. The dermis secretes the proteins collagen and elastin, which give support and elasticity to the skin. There are also immune cells in the dermis that defend against infectious agents that pass through the epidermis.

11.2.3 Subcutaneous Layer

The Subcutaneous layer is the innermost skin layer ("subcutaneous" meaning beneath the skin). This layer contains fat and muscle responsible for insulation and hydration of the skin.

11.3 The Purpose of Hair

Dogs' hair serves as a barrier between the fragile sensitive skin of the dog and the (potential damaging) environment. The dog's coat serves the following purposes: -

Tel: 01283 703043 Email: liza@heavenlyz.com

- Shielding from Ultraviolet sun damage, chemicals and other irritants such as plant pollen
- Prevents skin damage from accidental injury from thorns from bushes and other penetrable objects
- Helps regulate body temperature by trapping dead air space between secondary hairs and thereby conserving heat. This requires that the hairs be dry and waterproof. The cold-weather coat of many dogs is longer and finer to facilitate heat conservation. The hair of the coat can also help cool the skin. The warm-weather coat has shorter, thicker hairs and fewer secondary hairs. This anatomic change allows air to move easily through the coat, which facilitates cooling. This is the key reason why removal of double coated breeds such as Samoyeds is avoided.
- Dogs primarily release excess body heat by panting and drooling via the respiratory system (though dogs also have sweat glands on the feet that may have a minor role in cooling of the body)

11.4 Hair Parts

Hair can be divided into the following parts: -

- **Hair Shaft** – the part of the hair visible above the skin surface
- **Hair Follicle/ Root** – embedded in the dermis surface. The shape of the hair is determined by the shape of the follicle. Straight follicles produce straight hair and curly follicles produce curly hair.
- **Sebaceous gland** – responsible for secreting sebum (a mixture of fatty acids) which acts as a lubricant, weather proofing the coat and giving a lustrous appearance**.** The Sebaceous glands are especially prevalent in dogs near the paws, back of the neck, rump, chin, and tail area (hence why you may need to pay more attention to these areas when bathing). Sebum is also important for keeping the skin soft, moist, and pliable and it also has antibiotic properties.

11.5 Structure of Hair

If you were to cut a hair and look at the exposed end under a microscope, you would find the following: -

- **Cuticle**: the outermost layer of the hair is a single layer of flattened, keratinized cells overlapping like shingles or roof tiles that can be crown-like, petal-like or flat.
- **Cortex**: inside the cuticle is the intermediate, thickest, area. The dead keratinized cells are very densely packed. These cells contain pigment granules, providing the hair colour.
- **Medulla**: a central core of loosely packed cells. Hairs can be hollow, increasing the insulation value of the coat.

11.6 Hair Growth

The growth of hair is affected by nutrition, hormones, and change of season. Dogs normally shed hair in early spring and early autumn. Hair may also shed in response to changes in temperature or amount of sunlight. Disease, drugs and environment also affect the health of hair.

Hair grows in cycles. Its growth length is determined by the dog's genetic profile and/ or breed characteristics. Once the hair reaches this predetermined length, growing stops. Each growth cycle consists of four phases: anagen, catagen, telogen and exogen. The duration of each phase and the rate of hair growth determine the length and amount of coat on an individual dog.

11.6.1 Anagen (Growth Phase)

The anagen phase is the first phase of new hair growth. The cells in the bulb or base of the follicle produce new hair which pushes the old hair up the follicle to shed. Dogs such as poodles that do not tend to shed heavily have a longer anagen phase.

Dogs that continuously shed hair have shorter anagen phases. The amount of time the hair follicle stays in the anagen phase is genetically determined. At the end of the anagen phase, an unknown signal causes the follicle to go into the catagen phase.

11.6.2 Catagen (Regressing Phase)

The catagen phase is the transition phase. The catagen phase begins when the cell creation signals to stop hair growing during this phase.

11.6.3 Telogen (Rest Phase)

Telogen is a rest period between the catagen and anagen phases.

11.6.4 Exogen (Shedding Phase)

The final phase, exogen, is the shedding phase. This phase occurs when the hair falls out and the follicle moves back into the anagen phase. The length of this phase depends on the season.

11.7 Hair growth cycle

At any given moment, some hair follicles are in anagen, some in catagen and some in telogen. The timing and the ratio of the different cycles determine the shedding frequency, the length of the hair and presence or absence of undercoat. Some dogs shed poorly because almost all their follicles are in anagen (growth stage) almost all the time, so their hair just gets longer and longer. Some dogs have most of their follicles in telogen (rest stage) and they may be almost completely hairless. Hair growth rate varies between individual dogs and even between the different anatomical regions in the same dog. The growth rate is generally most rapid in the shoulder region, followed by the flank and the forehead regions of the dog.

11.8 Hair Types

The following hair types are relevant to dogs: -

- **Guard Hairs** (primary hairs) form the topcoat, the outermost layer of hair that covers most of the skin surface. They are thick, long and stiff. The guard hairs are regularly arranged in broad tracts that follow the contour of the body and give the animal's coat its smooth appearance. Growing one hair per primary follicle, the guard hair provides a waterproof protective top layer covering the undercoat. Guard hairs are most abundant on the back of the animal.
- **Under-Hairs** form the undercoat (secondary hairs). They are thin, short and soft. They give the coat its softness and provide insulation.
- **Tactile Hair** – e.g. Whiskers/ eye lashes. These are very large hairs, genetically evolved specifically to act as mechanical sensors. They are thicker than topcoat or undercoat hair, but they have the same structure. Note that tactile hairs are deeply embedded, growing from a special hair follicle incorporating a capsule of blood. DO NOT CUT TACTILE HAIR.

11.9 Hair Shedding

Shedding should not be viewed as sudden hair loss, but should be considered as the best indicator of the health of the skin and hair of the dog. Coat gloss, hair softness, a greasy or dry feeling to the coat and the presence of dandruff are also good indicators of the hair's condition. However, these factors are judged subjectively on an individual dog by dog basis. With a good understanding of the hair structure and characteristics, these health indicators will help you determine the status of the dog's hair and health condition. This is important to enable the professional groomer to be able to detect abnormalities when a dog is presented to them in the salon.

Tel: 01283 703043 Email: liza@heavenlyz.com

11.10 Alopecia (Spontaneous hair loss)

The following table identifies a few common ailments and conditions that may lead to the development of hair loss or bald patches on a dog's coat (this table is not intended to cover all ailments; other hair loss conditions may be found in the salon): -

	Name of ailment	Cause	Signs/ Symptoms	Diagnosis/ Treatment	Health considerations
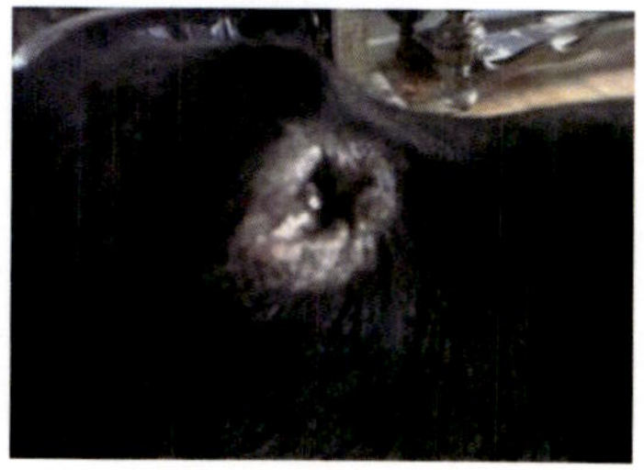	Demodicosis	Demodex mite	Mites multiply within the follicle, leading to generalised hair loss seen especially around eyes, ears and face.	Requires veterinary attention.	If cause for skin thickening or hair loss unknown, wear PPE as mites are Zoonotic, Secondary bacterial pyoderma may be a problem
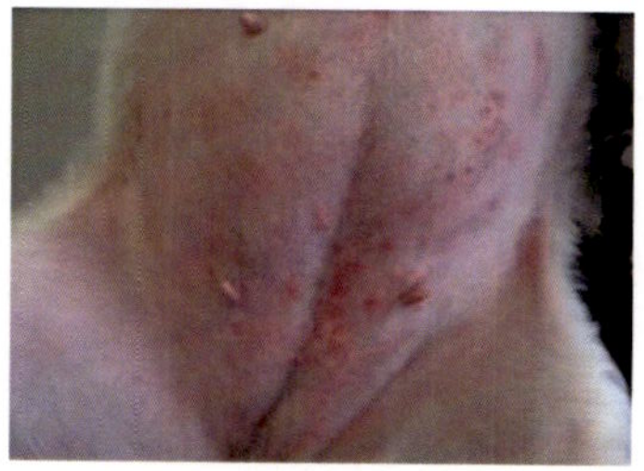	"Superficial staphylococcal folliculitis" or "Secondary bacterial pyoderma"	Bacterial	Generalised small pustule lesions on skin confined usually to groin area and rarely seen on face, feet or limbs	Veterinary prescribed antibiotics and addressing underlying cause	Maintain good salon hygiene and clean equipment between uses.
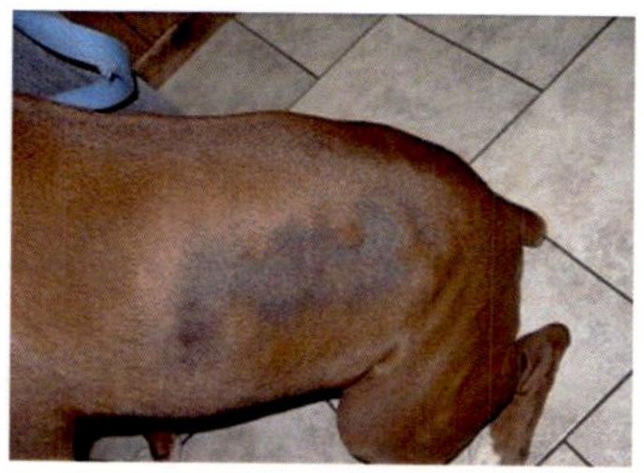	Endocrine diseases	Thyroid or hormonal imbalance.	The three most common endocrine disorders to affect a dog's skin are (i) hypothyroidism, (ii) hyperadrenocorticism (Cushing's disease) and (iii) oestrogen- and testosterone-producing tumours, resulting in abnormal sex hormone concentrations.	Hair loss is noticeable, predominately down the dogs back, flanks and tail and requires veterinary investigation	Protect exposed hairless Skin from potential harmful UV sunrays. Support treatment.

Tel: 01283 703043 Email: liza@heavenlyz.com

	Name of ailment	Cause	Signs/ Symptoms	Diagnosis/ Treatment	Health considerations
	Post-clipping alopecia	Removal of coat (commonly seen in sled dog breeds)	Likely to be due to clipping of hair when all the hairs are synchronised in the telogen phase (resting phase) and it usually resolves following subsequent growth phases (anagen phase)	Discuss alternate method to clipping with Client	The importance of written consent to remove a double coated breed at owners' request is advisable as permanent coat damage may be caused
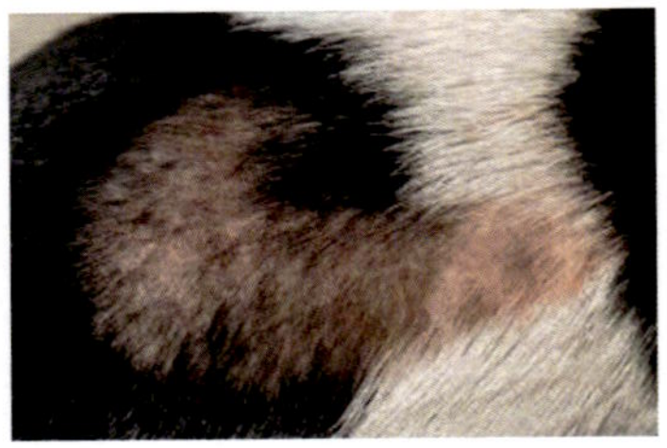	Stress	Stressful events, high fever, pregnancy/ lactation, shock, severe illness, surgery or anaesthesia	Anaesthesia can cause abrupt cessation of growth in anagen hair follicles, resulting in many hair follicles being synchronised in the telogen phase. Two to three months later, a new wave of follicular activity begins and all the telogen hairs are shed leading to temporary alopecia. This phenomenon is known as telogen defluxion.	If normal hair growth does not resume after several months veterinary advise should be sought	Protect exposed hairless Skin from potential harmful U.V sunrays. Support treatment.
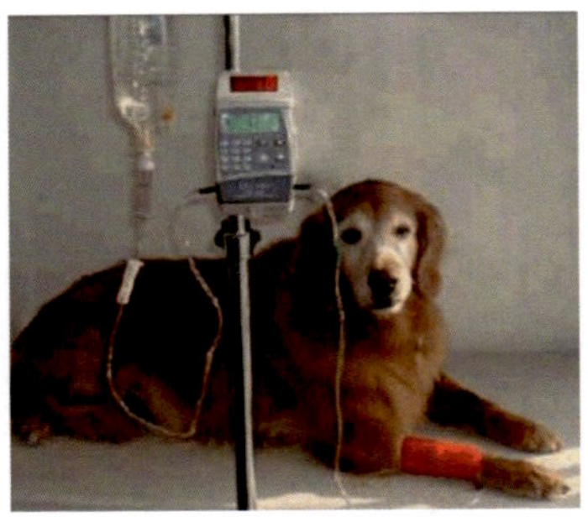	Cancer	Certain drugs Chemotherapy	Certain drugs can influence the hair bulb (e.g. stopping all growth). The weakened hair shaft then breaks off below the surface resulting in a phenomenon known as anagen defluxion.	When the drug therapy or chemotherapy stops, the hair will regrow at the next cycle.	PPE (wear gloves) There is risk of carcinogenic here. Mandatory if the owner requires that a chemotherapy tablet be given whilst dog in your care.

Email: liza@heavenlyz.com

	Name of ailment	Cause	Signs/ Symptoms	Diagnosis/ Treatment	Health considerations
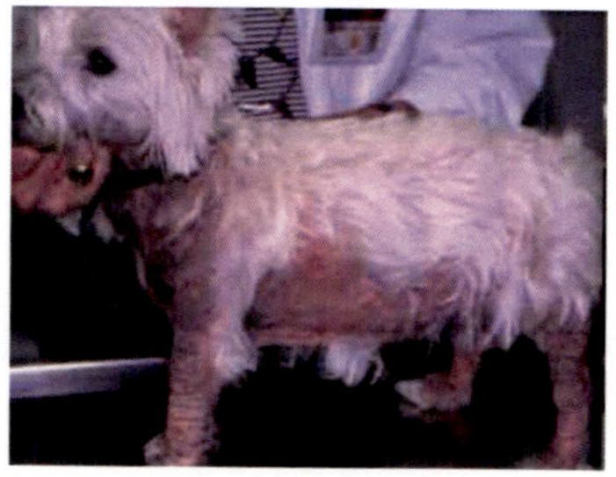	Auto-immune disease	Unknown - many theories exist including (i) over vaccination, (ii) environmental pollutants, (iii) food preservatives found in most dog foods, (iv) genetics	Autoimmune disease is an immune system failure where the body begins to attack itself, rejecting the body's own tissue as foreign. In this disease, activated lymphocytes attack certain components of the hair follicle and bulb leading to possible irreversible alopecia.	Consult with Veterinary Surgeon	Veterinary support and management
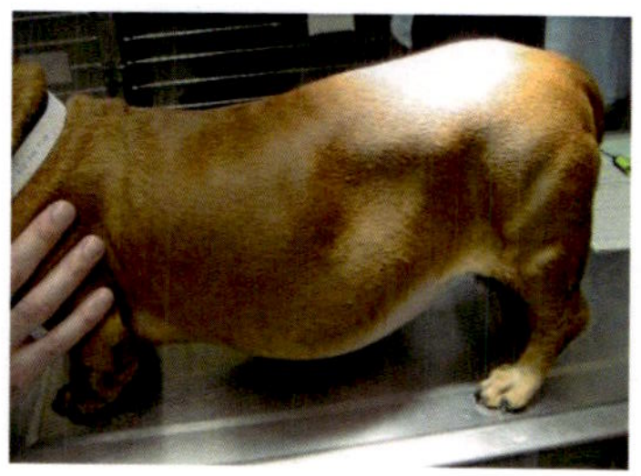	Cushings disease/ Hyperadrenocorticism	About 85 percent of cases are caused by a tumour in the pituitary gland, while 15 percent are caused by an adrenal tumour. The pituitary gland produces a hormone that signals the adrenal gland to produce cortisol; a tumour can cause it to produce the adrenal-stimulating hormone even when it is not needed. Cushing's can be caused by overuse of steroid medications; in some cases,	Characterized by an increase in glucocorticoids secreted by the adrenal glands. Signs include increased appetite, increased drinking and urination, a pot-bellied appearance, muscle weakness, and lethargy	Diagnosis can be difficult as there are no tests with both high sensitivity and specificity. Stopping the medication is enough to solve the problem. Treatments include mitotane, trilostane, ketoconazole, or selegiline. Surgery is used in some cases of adrenal tumours.	

Tel: 01283 703043 Email: liza@heavenlyz.com

	Name of ailment	Cause	Signs/ Symptoms	Diagnosis/ Treatment	Health considerations
	Addisons disease/	All causes are not yet known. Usual causes are genetic, often related to autoimmune disorders. Other cases are caused by various disease processes.	Primary signs: Lethargy, anorexia, vomiting, weight loss, and weakness. Secondary signs: dehydration, bradycardia, weak femoral pulses, abdominal pain. Occasional reports: Polyuria and polydipsia, diarrhoea, and shivering.	Monthly injections of fludrocortisone (trade name Florinef) or Percorten-V (desoxycorticosterone pivalate, DOCP) and prednisolone or Zycortal. Routine blood work is undertaken until maintenance dose is established. Most medications used cause excessive thirst and urination (even more vital to provide fresh drinking water).	Dosage may be increased for stressful situations – e.g. travel.
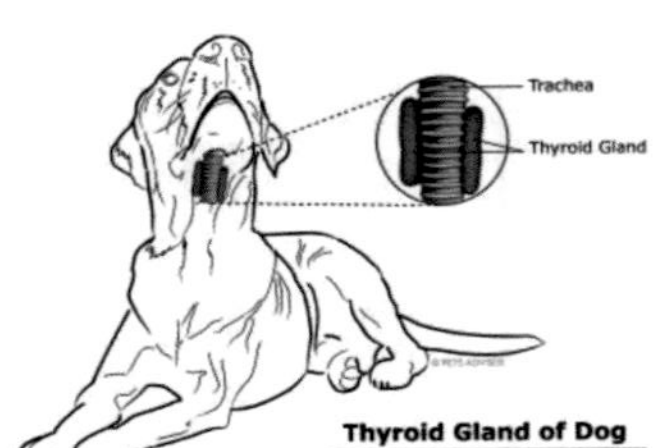	Hyper Thyroid	Auto-immune issues Thyroid nodules (increases size and production of gland) Thyroid cancer	Symptoms are progressive: - • skin disease • weight gain • inactivity • intolerance to cold temperatures • hair may thin & shed excessively • skin may dry and flake • potential tendency toward bacterial skin infections	Surgical removal of thyroid tumours Radiation therapy	

Email: liza@heavenlyz.com

12 Canine Body Language

Before a dog groom is attempted, the dog's temperament should be assessed for behaviour and the best method/ approach to handling should be decided. The following are typical behaviours that the dog may demonstrate whilst in your care at some stage of their visit to your salon. It is important to be able to understand each behaviour such that communication with the dog is enhanced and the needs of the dog are supported.

12.1 Happy

The dog will seem relaxed, calm and may wag tail.

12.2 Playful

A playful dog is happy and excited. Ears may be held up, alert, eyes will be bright, and the tail may wag rapidly. The dog may bounce around and play bow.

12.3 Submissive

A submissive dog holds head down low, ears lie flat to head and eyes averted. Tail is low and may sway slightly but is not tucked. They may roll over onto back and expose belly. A submissive dog may also nuzzle or lick handler.

12.4 Anxious

Takes on a submissive stance, may whimper, yawn, lick lips. Tail may be low, may be tucked and may be over sensitive to stimuli. This state can lead to fearful aggression.

12.5 Fearful

The fearful dog combines submissive and anxious behaviour and may display more extreme signals. Stance may be tense, the body low to ground, the ears flat to back and the eyes narrow and averted. The tail may be between legs and whole body can tremble. A fearful dog may growl and show teeth, occasionally urinating and defecating. A fearful dog can turn aggressive very quickly if threatened.

12.6 Dominant

A dominant dog will try and assert themselves over other dogs and occasionally people. The dog will stand tall, confident and may lean forward to assert themselves. Ears will be pricked, and the dog may growl slow and low.

12.7 Aggressive

An aggressive dog goes far beyond dominance. All feet are firmly planted on ground in a territorial manner, and they may lunge forward. Ears are pinned back, head straight and eyes are narrow and piercing. Tail held up high, even slow wagging, baring teeth, snapping jaw, barking threateningly. The hairs along back and scruff stand on edge.

Tel: 01283 703043 Email: liza@heavenlyz.com

13 Handling, Restraint & Moving dogs around the salon

Caution: some dogs' behaviour deteriorates when restraint methods are applied – remember that dogs' good behaviour is promoted where over-handling is avoided.

As a dog groomer, we need to have knowledge and understanding of signs of stress and how different temperaments of dogs may present themselves to us, for us to be able to work safely and without causing undue stress to our colleagues, other animals in the salon and the dogs we are working with.

The dog groomer should always adopt a positive manner. Remain confident when approaching a dog, be firm but kind, this will help the dog recognise that you are in charge. Consider that underlying medical problems may or may not be known to the owner (e.g. underlying heart complaints). Stress and anxiety can cause these problems to worsen during the dog's time in the salon.

It's important to maximise praise of well-behaved dogs and to limit negativity when communicating with the dog. Attempt to ignore bad behaviour as much as reasonably possible. Remember that it is far better to not start a groom or stop a groom midway rather than endanger humans or dogs. Know your own limitations and always ask for help or advice if you are unsure. Any of the following behaviours mean the dog could bite: -

- Growling
- Snarling
- Curling lips
- Lunging
- Snapping
- Barking aggressively

If a dog shows any of these signs whilst grooming, you must be firm but fair. You **SHOULD NOT** be rough. **DO NOT USE** grooming tools to correct bad behaviour by distraction (e.g. by banging the table with a brush) – this could not only damage the equipment, but the dog could also associate the tool with discipline or relate it to the unwanted behaviour, which in turn will make them even more fearful with the grooming process...the circle of bad behaviour continues.

If the dog continues with the unwanted behaviour and there is a chance that the dog may bite, a muzzle may be necessary alongside the use of the "Groomer's Helper".

Observe safety when using a muzzle or restraint. Only use if dogs breed anatomy (i.e. head shape) will permit and where no medical conditions will be contravened. All dogs must be under close observation and never left unattended where a muzzle or restraint is in place.

Confirm the dog's temperament by checking the record card and by seeking advice from their owner.

Place an appropriate salon 'slip lead' on all dogs (confirm correct rope diameter and correct fitment to avoid damage to dog's throat).

Avoid kennelling a stressed or aggressive dog wearing a slip lead where possible. If the dog must be kennelled, leave the lead trailing out under the door to keep you safe when moving the dog from the crate as some dogs may 'guard' the kennel/ crate. **Caution....** constantly observe to avoid accidental strangulation.

Advice: Learn to discriminate between signs of fear and signs of aggression.

Establishing a routine within the salon will help reduce anxiety. Have the same stylist handle the dog from start to finish, avoid long intervals between treatments, make the grooming environment as quiet, calm and relaxed as possible.

13.1 Behaviours

Visual signs of typical or normal behaviours that dogs exhibit: -

- Panting (but not excessively)
- Barking (but not excessively)
- Drinking
- Eating
- Self-cleaning (but not excessive licking)
- Rest
- Play
- Socialisation
- Territory marking
- Sniffing, but let's elaborate on "sniffing". The area of the canine brain that processes scent analysis scent is 40 times greater than that of the human. Dogs can identify smells at least 1,000 times better than humans. Dogs' noses have 220 million olfactory receptors, compared to a human's "tiny" 5 million - it's no wonder that smell is the dog's primary sense. When a dog sniffs, air is taken in and passes through nasal skin cells. These cells are also found in the Jacobsen's or vomeronasal organ, which human's do not have. The Jacobsen's organ is thought to be important in detection of

Tel: 01283 703043 Email: liza@heavenlyz.com

pheromones/ body scents, perhaps this is the reason why dogs have a heightened ability to identify/ recognise animals and people.

Atypical visual signs or potentially abnormal behaviours that dogs exhibit: -

- Destructive behaviour
- Aggression
- Increased drinking defecating and urination
- Fighting
- Submission
- Coprophagia (consumption of faeces – whether own or another beings)

13.2 Signs of fear, anxiety and stress in a dog

The dog backs away from you, cowers or puts its tail between its legs.

The dog averts their gaze, yawns, licks their lips, moves slowly (almost slow-motion-like) or acts sleepy when they should be wide awake.

Excessive panting/ actual physically shaking and involuntary passing of urine or faeces.

Ears held back, sweating paws, coughing/hacking

Caution: a raised lip or a sudden tense frozen posture, accompanied by the dog exhibiting several the above warning signs may result in a bite.

13.3 What causes change in behaviour

Behavioural changes can be caused by several reasons, including: -

- Separation from another dog or human
- Dog suffering pain
- Dog in season
- History of dog e.g. rescue, lack of socialisation
- Breed specific- coward collie etc

13.4 General Grooming Behavioural Considerations

The professional animal carer should consider each animal as an individual (e.g. never assume that because it's a Golden Cocker Spaniel it will behave like the Golden Cocker Spaniels you have cared for before).

Take time to get to know the dog as an individual to understand where that dog's boundaries and level of tolerance lie, and work to not over step these boundaries.

If applied correctly, the typical animal carer/ animal relationship has potential to last over a decade. It is best to kick off the first meeting well, by showing respect and understanding for the animal. Heavenlyz recommends grooming appointment systems that default to at least 2.5 hours for each dog treatment – observing this will help the experience to be stress free and positive for both groomer and dog.

Ensure though that you have sufficient contingency time to allow you to carry out the groom in a planned and professional manner. If you make a mistake or the animal presents a difficulty that had not previously been identified, then explain to the owner the reasons why you require more time to carry out the service. Reschedule for a time when the service will not be rushed, and you have the necessary resources and expertise to complete the treatment.

Many dogs with special needs require frequent comfort breaks, modification of handling and appropriate/ safe use of restraints. The service may have to be undertaken in stages. All this takes time, sometimes longer than the planned schedule. This may incur greater cost or require the client to work with you in ways that they did not expect. In neither you nor the client can agree on the best way to service the animal, then you as the supplier are quite entitled to decline to provide that service on animal health grounds.

13.5 Specific Conditions/ Situations impacting the Grooming Process

The following conditions are a few of the most common that would impact the dog grooming process.

13.5.1 Brachycephalic breeds

These are short-nosed (e.g. Bulldogs/ Pugs). These breeds have bulging eyes and should not be scruffed or restrained excessively as their eyes may prolapse (i.e. exit the eye socket). These breeds find breathing more difficult, can suffer from heat stress/ stroke very easily and care needs to be taken whilst restraining in order not to exacerbate their difficulties. In the case of these breeds, proper application of a towel or Elizabethan collar can aid restraint.

13.5.2 Chondrodysplastic breeds

These are long-bodied/ short-legged breeds (e.g. Bassett hounds, Dachshunds). Care must be taken lifting these breeds as they are prone to disc and back problems. You must support the whole body or ask for support. Use two people to lift a heavy breed like the Bassett hound.

13.5.3 Juveniles/ Toy Dogs

These dogs are delicate and extra care is needed when handling, especially where lifting their legs, etc. These breeds can be more excitable. Take care to ensure that they don't jump out of your arms when being carried. Patience is required with the very young.

13.5.4 Geriatric Dogs

Take care with geriatric animals (who may be partially sighted or hard of hearing). Ensure the salon walkways are clear of obstructions to avoid the dog accidentally banging into objects, a level floor will help prevent trips or falls.

If a crating policy is in operation within the salon, geriatrics are best housed in a floor level crate with adequate bedding.

Plan for extra care when handling elderly dogs, which may feel pain when lifting legs due to arthritis and other pre-existing conditions such as hip dysplasia.

Old dogs require gentle handling and should be allowed to move at their own pace. They may have heart complaints, arthritis, respiratory or other problems. Some of these pets may be deaf, blind or even a little senile, make sure they are well restrained on the table.

Speak gently and reassure them throughout grooming process.

If in a cage/ kennel these pets may sleep deeply and not hear you, so make sure you make noise before attempting to touch them if sleeping, as a startled dog may bite.

13.5.5 Pregnant Dogs.

It may not be ideal to groom a pregnant bitch. However, if safe to do so or medical grounds apply (e.g. rescue bitch has mange or pelted coat), these dogs can be groomed with extra care. Avoid stress, groom these dogs at an end of day appointment where you can commit your attention to one dog and the usual salon noise levels will be reduced further. Ensure the dog is supported throughout. DO NOT put your hand under the stomach to lift, employ a scoop or calf-lift technique or perhaps even groom on the floor. Ensure adequate breaks.

13.5.6 Extra-large dogs.

These dogs will be heavy! When lifting a large breed of dog, it may require 2 persons.

13.5.7 Post-operative dogs.

The best treatment for post-operative dog is, if possible, is invariably NOT to groom a post-operative dog.

It is far better to arrange a schedule with the owner to groom the dog immediately before the operation/ procedure as possible. This will allow the maximum time after operation/ procedure before a groom is required.

If this is unavoidable (e.g. unplanned emergencies) then please make sure you have complete understanding of the injury/ recovering illness and consider doing the groom in stages.

Contact the vet treating the dog before treatment begins and, on their advice,, ensure the salon is as safe as possible.

Perhaps elect to groom first thing in the morning or during quiet periods where floors are drier/ more non-slip and there is little chance of the excitement of having other dogs around. You are trying to avoid boisterous behaviour, keep restraint easy and prevent excitement.

Tel: 01283 703043 Email: liza@heavenlyz.com

As with all grooms, ensure bath and table non-slip to prevent slips/ strains and make use of hydraulics/ electrics/ ramps/ steps to avoid jumping on and off the table/bath.

13.5.8 Wounded Dogs

It is advisable not to get the wound sutures wet so keep the operation site dry always

13.5.9 Deaf Dogs

A dog with hearing impairment will rely more on their other senses such as smell and sight. Ensure that when you approach a deaf dog you approach from the front, in plain sight, that you understand that the dog can see you and that make your intentions very clear through slow, precise, body language movements. This is intended to avoid any confusion on the part of the dog. Never startle a dog in a housing unit, especially a disabled dog (e.g. deafness). You need to work to ensure that you avoid the 'flight or fight' reflex occurring within the dog, which may mean that the dog could bolt or bite you.

13.5.10 Blind/ Partially Sighted Dogs

This group of dogs includes those who are completely blind, those who may have partial sight (e.g. Cataracts).

Ensure that this type of dog is guided around the salon on a short lead and encouraged to keep close to your leg. It is worth asking clients on which side they walk their dogs. Although many professional handlers walk dogs of the left, if the pet's owner walks the dog on the right, then this could lead to confusion. Remain consistent to help dog feel secure whilst in the salon with you.

Ensure floor surfaces are level as far as practically possible, try to avoid stairs. If your premises operate on more than level, then guide the dog sufficiently to avoid confidence damaging trips or stumbles – the dog's confidence in its handlers and surroundings will enhance the grooming outcome.

A sight-damaged dog's housing should be on ground floor level. Ensure that you show the dog where they can find the water bowl etc. Ensure that the housing for that dog remains exclusive for that dog only for the complete duration in your care. Avoid allowing other dogs to sleep on bedding or scent the area. Keep all enrichments (e.g. water bowls) in same place. It's worth making a note of where you place the water bowl and what cage the dog prefers so you can always house the dog in the same unit – this will provide continuity and enhance the confidence of the dog.

13.5.11 Limb Incapacitation/ Loss

Ensure the surfaces of your premises are non-slip. You may assist the dog in their movement (e.g. assisted blanket walking, where a soft material is rolled and placed gently under the area of incapacity and where the handler uses that material to support (or help support) the dog's weight.

Ensure that this type of dog is not standing for long periods of time, give the dog plenty of breaks and ensure that any restraint is appropriate to the incapacity and that it properly supports the dog's body weight without pain or discomfort to the dog.

Avoid lifting good legs that compensate for the incapacity as this may place too much strain on other legs. If you need to lift legs (e.g. feet scissoring) then encourage the dog to sit or lie down.

13.5.12 Arthritis and other joint pain/ disorders

A dog's leg should never be lifted higher than the joint to which it is attached. For example, foot no higher than ankle or hock joint. Dogs with problematic joints may suffer pain and discomfort through any movement. Try and position yourself around the dog as opposed to positioning the dog around you. Allow the dog to sit or lie in whatever position is comfortable to them. Ensure regular breaks throughout the groom.

13.5.13 Cardiac/ Heart Problems

Heart murmurs occur due to turbulence in the blood flow (for whatever reason) making heartbeat irregular. Dependant of the severity of the murmurs, the dog may present few signs. The dog may be extremely fatigued (much more so and much more easily than fit and healthy dogs). The dog may present excessive panting and quickened pulse. For any disabled dog, assessments and actions should be considered on a case by case basis but the main considerations in this instance are (i) to provide a well ventilated, cool, environment throughout the grooming process, (ii) avoid over exerting the dog – remember, this type of dog will be able to do less, (iii) provide increased potential for breaks and (iv) avoid stressing the dog/ raising blood pressure.

Quicker, more frequent grooming visits are suggested for familiarisation (to avoid stress) and the over use of restraints are to be avoided.

Tel: 01283 703043 Email: liza@heavenlyz.com

13.5.14 Syringomyelia

Syringomyelia is a hereditary problem mainly affecting pedigree Cavalier King Charles Spaniels (though other breeds can also be affected). The condition presents as a fluid-filled sac on the spinal cord, usually due to malformation of the brain and the bones of the skull. The condition is congenital, and much more likely to occur in small dogs than larger ones, due to their smaller skull size and conformation in general.

Syringomyelia is a chronic condition and degenerates progressively in affected dogs. It often causes intense pain and headaches, as well as stiffness in the neck, back and limbs. It can also cause weakness and numbness in the limbs, and a range of other potential effects including loss of bladder or bowel control and an inability to regulate the body temperature, and overheating.

To help dogs with this condition, make surfaces non-slip, ensure noise levels are kept to a minimum (the use of a happy hoody could help reduce noise for dog when drying).

Overheating is particularly bad with this condition so dry the dog as quickly as possible in a well ventilated, low temperature room. Use a blaster to remove most moisture before stand drying. Remain observant and monitor for overheating. Signs of overheating can include excessive salivation, red mucous membranes/ eyes/ mouth and excessive panting.

Consider grooming the dog in stages interrupted by periods of rest.

13.6 Controlled movement around the salon

Control the dog's movement. Avoid chasing the dog or letting the dog pace – scenarios like this will cause the dog to become more anxious, excited, or aroused and consequently more likely to bite.

Calmly control movement by keeping an appropriate and consistent leash length. The leash should be long enough so there's no pressure on the dog when it's stationary but short enough to keep the dog from pacing on the table top.

It is advisable not to let dogs loose/ free-roam around the salon. This is a health and safety concern, as injuries could occur due to falling equipment, dog fights or groomers tripping over loose dogs.

13.7 Initial approach

If the dog is aggressive when the owner is present or when you take the dog off the owner, ask the owner to place the dog on a slip lead.

Owners of aggressive dogs should be requested to wait in reception whilst you remove the dog from the protection of the owner. Once removed from the owner, the dog should begin to behave but only once the dog is established should the owner leave the salon.

Try and plan precisely for pickup time in this instance and ensure that the owner knows to return punctually at the agreed time, to avoid having the dog waiting in the salon for a long time.

Note that a “head-on” approach with/ without an outstretched arm can force a fearful dog to feel like it must defend itself! A more appropriate approach is to stand or crouch sideways, avert your gaze, and let the dog make first contact. For a fearful dog, approach from the side – as approaching from the front can be seen as a threat.

Speak in a happy, high-pitched, fun, non-threatening, voice. Having checked that the dog is not on a strict diet, potentially offer a small treat to attempt to change the dog's perception.

Avoid hugging or placing your face to the face of an unfamiliar dog. Whilst some dogs may tolerate being hugged, few dogs enjoy it. Even a friendly dog may bite when an unfamiliar person invades its personal space in this manner.

13.8 Training/ Shaping and diversion techniques

Forcibly restraining dogs for procedures such as a nail trim can make the dog more fearful or reactive each time you try (i.e. the dog can become more aggressive). Avoid holding animals down for handling procedures.

Instead, take the time to train the dog to tolerate handling, we call this ‘shaping’ behaviour. Shaping behaviour is not instant and may be required over several visits

Dogs can be trained to tolerate regular handling procedures such as grooming & nail trims, often in a very short amount of time. Groomer and owner should work together, a grooming plan should be drawn up which rewards good behaviour and reinforces the positive grooming experience.

Tel: 01283 703043 Email: liza@heavenlyz.com

Heavenlyz recommends that a dog who demonstrates a fearful aggression towards grooming attends the salon on a regular basis. This is done for the dog to be groomed 'little and often'.

Heavenlyz recommends diversion techniques. These can be carried out with careful planning to ensure the diversion is appropriate for the dog. Always understand the dog's dietary limitations and get owners consent before using food treats as a diversion as the dog may have an intolerance to food sources and/ or may be on a calorie-controlled diet.

Diversions from the grooming process may include: -

- an appropriate toy filled with a dog-attractive, edible, substance
- the dogs favourite toy given to them each time they have demonstrated patience and tolerance.

13.9 Restraint

13.9.1 Manual Restraint

When restraining or repositioning a dog, ensure that a non-slip surface (for both you and the dog) is in place and that you're supporting the animal.

If pressure is placed in the wrong anatomical areas or where the dog does not feel secure, this can be counter-productive and make a well-behaved animal start to struggle/ become aggressive.

Consider whether you need an assistant to help you with the restraint of a large or aggressive dog. Avoid working alone with large and aggressive breeds.

13.9.2 Safety considerations for a restrained dog.

To be groomed, a dog needs to feel (and be) safe and secure.

NEVER leave a dog unattended on the table or in the bath.

ALWAYS keep one of your hands on the dog when in the bath or on the table.

REMEMBER before removing a dog from the grooming table remove the neck strap – failing to do so can cause injury.

Harnesses can be used to restrain dogs (a) with neck/ back injuries, (b) with long-bodies, (c) with collapsing trachea syndrome or (d) which lean and choke on a direct neck restraint.

Always ask for assistance if you are unsure how to handle a dog.

13.9.3 Equipment supported restraint

Never leave a dog unattended on the table even if adequately restrained.

If a direct neck restraint is required, ensure it has an appropriate, anti-choke, quick release mechanism. Avoid knot-ties on leads. These can be difficult to free, especially when a dog is struggling. Dogs may get themselves into an accidental choke situation or even hang themselves.

If necessary, use a belly strap to prevent the dog from spinning round, sitting down or sliding off the table - this prevents constantly having to lift the dog up which can annoy some dogs and lead to our own fatigue and injury.

As with all restraints less is more, try to avoid using them throughout the entire groom and only use when necessary.

Belly strap - a good belly strap should be made from padded, water proof, material which will not cause any friction burns when in situ. The belly strap is for support only. Please ensure that it is not too tight causing unnecessary distress on the dog. The strap is to help the dog support its own bodyweight, all four feet should be allowed to be firmly planted on a non-slip table surface, the table should be stable enough not to rock and the frame supporting the strap large enough/ fixed correctly such that it will not collapse under the weight of the dog. A loose frame risks injury to the dog and you will have great difficulties trying to convince the dog to join you and cooperate again with you next time. Remember, we must ensure the safety of the dogs always.

Groomers helpers - are commercially available and come in two parts, one supporting the belly of the dog and the other sufficiently locating the dog's head to the A-frame whilst still allowing the dog to bend or flex its head. Heavenlyz recommend these only to be used in extreme circumstances and not for every day grooming. However, it depends of your approach to restraint, Heavenlyz approach is, with the possible exception of the quick release neck strap, to use restraint only when needed.

Tel: 01283 703043 Email: liza@heavenlyz.com

Hammocks - used to support whole body to include chest and abdomen and are commercial available. Care should be taken to ensure all four feet stay well planted and firm on the table to ensure the dogs feels supported but also to ensure the dogs back remains in the correct position. Some groomers are using these products with dog suspended in the hammock, Heavenlyz does not recommend this. However, if you wish to use this technique, you must ensure that the dog's back remains straight (not "banana'd") and that the dog is not being forced into a restraint position which could cause potential both mental and physical injury.

Buster collars - available in solid plastic traditional cone type (known as an "Elizabethan collar") and now also available in portable, easy to use inflatable types. Dogs prefer the latter type; this equipment is a great alternative to muzzling particularly with short nosed breeds.

Muzzles - A muzzle could worsen behaviour. Muzzles attract a risk of over-heating as they make it more difficult for the dog to regulate its own body temperature through effective panting and respiration. Muzzles can also cause vomiting or asphyxiation!

13.9.4 Muzzles

Muzzles are worthy of special note - careful consideration is required before placing a muzzle on a dog: -

- Does the dog have an underlying medical condition (e.g. heart condition, epileptic, etc.) which could be exaggerated by muzzling?
- Is the muzzle suitable for the size and face shape of the dog?

If a muzzle must be applied, ensure it applied correctly and securely and observe the following: -

- Do not leave a muzzle on for long periods of time.
- Do not place the dog in a drying cabinet where a muzzle is applied.
- Do not leave an animal unattended when it is wearing a muzzle.

The following sections identify the common types of muzzles that are currently commercially available.

13.9.4.1 Box/ Basket muzzle

See "Figure 1 - Box/ basket muzzle". This muzzle is structured like a wire box or basket muzzle and has excellent air flow, allowing the dog more comfort. This is especially useful for short nosed breeds but is also suitable for Mesocephalic head shape breeds (e.g. Labrador/ Beagle)

Figure 1 - Box/ basket muzzle

Figure 2 - Nylon muzzle

13.9.4.2 Nylon Muzzle

See Figure 2 - Nylon muzzle. This muzzle is available in a variety of sizes and it should be noted that they restrict the dog's ability to pant. It is suitable for **Dolichocephalic** head shape breeds (e.g. Rough Collie/ Saluki).

Tel: 01283 703043 Email: liza@heavenlyz.com

13.9.4.3 Elizabethan/ Buster collar

This type of collar is most useful for **Brachycephalic** type breeds (e.g. French bull dog/ Pug).

13.10 Lifting dogs

A dog should be lifted on to and off from a grooming table, always using the same method. **Never** allow a dog to jump down from the grooming table in case of slip/ fall injury.

13.10.1 Small and medium size dogs

Small and medium size dogs may need only one person to lift, but, if ever in doubt, use 2 people to lift a dog.

- Place your arm around dog's neck in front of the forelegs
- Place your other arm behind the dog's rump
- Gentle scoop to lift the dog, bending knee
- Use your knees to lift, never your back (keep your back straight during the lift)

13.10.2 Large dogs

Lifting large dogs requires two people.

- Person one; places arm around dog's neck in front of the forelegs whilst the second arm is placed under the dog's chest.
- Person two; places their arm under the dog's abdomen and the other arm under the rump.
- Both persons should bend from the knee to lift, whilst keeping their backs straight.

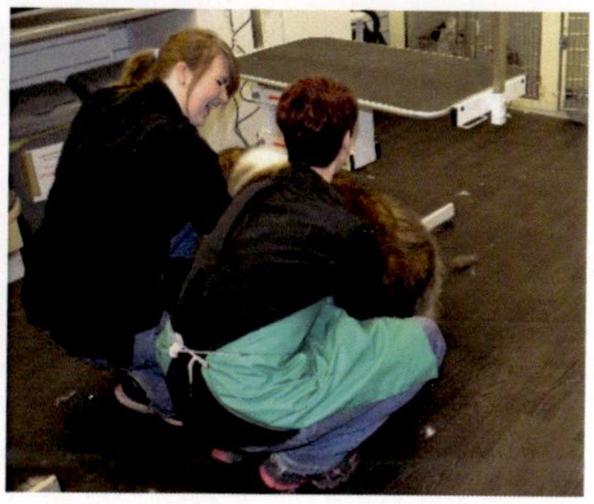

13.10.3 Use of ramp or steps

When working alone you may not be able to seek assistance to lift a large breed dog. It is not advisable for dogs to jump on or off the table because injury may occur. When handling a long back large breed such as Basset Hound, you cannot simply lower the table/ hydraulic bath and place the fore legs onto the target surface as this will still incur some twisting to the spine (to be avoided in long back breeds).

In all these instances it is better to have a series of portable steps or ramps in place.

Never force a dog up steps or ramp. Use gentle encouragement; avoid dragging, slipping or any other forceful movement which may cause potential damage (e.g. cruciate injuries).

13.11 Transporting Dogs

Many grooming salons offer a collection and delivery service. Those involved in the transportation of dogs should observe legislation/ the following guidelines, be properly trained and should design transportation procedures to suit their specific workplace.

Remember that, during transportation, pets should never be left unattended – this is especially important on warm days and critically important in Summer.

It is important to remember that the driver of the vehicle is legally responsible for the road safety of the vehicle, regardless of vehicle registration and ownership. In addition, ensure that the chosen vehicle is suitably prepared to carry pets as follows: -

- Plan the journey to allow for unforeseen circumstances (e.g. freedom to defecate/ urinate; traffic jam in hot weather).

Tel: 01283 703043 Email: liza@heavenlyz.com

- Ensure that you carry a suitable travel pack with you always – this could include water and a vessel within which to place the water, an animal first aid kit, additional leads, bedding and cleansing products.
- Confirm Vehicle is ready for travel (e.g. road tax, MOT, water for window screen cleaning, correct tyre pressure, all lights in working order, etc...).
- Dogs should not be transported loose, they can distract the driver and could cause an accident. Confirm that the vehicle is habitable for the animal and that it is equipped with well-maintained crates for transporting animals. Cages should be suitably sized such that the pet can comfortably stand up, turn around and lie down.
- Ensure dog's record card is carried and that it is up to date (e.g. correct address, etc.)

Tel: 01283 703043 Email: liza@heavenlyz.com

14 Grooming Techniques

Assuming the dog's temperament supports the groom taking place, various attributes including the dog's coat type, medical condition, lifestyle, etc., determines which of the following techniques should be used during the groom: -

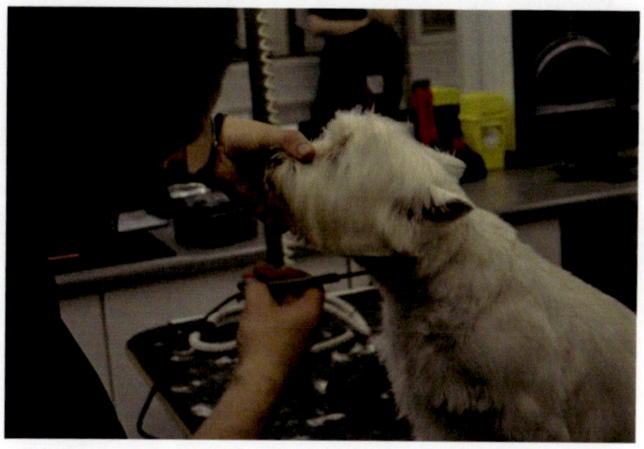

- Clipping
- Hygiene clipping
- Thinning
- Scissoring
- Handstripping
- Grooming out, deshedding and dematting

14.1 Clipping

This relates to the removal of live and dead coat with an electric or battery-operated clipper. Clipping can modify coat length depending on the clipper blade used. Attachment combs can also be used over the clipper blade to give a longer scissor look. Clipping can be carried out on all coat types, but is not recommended on double coated or smooth coated breeds unless instructed under veterinary advice.

When requested to clip double coated breeds - ask yourself "why?" Some owners request removal of a double coated hair during the summer months to keep the dog cool. This is a misconception. Providing the dog's coat is in good condition with no matts, felting or pelting, it will act effectively and efficiently as an insulator **against** both hot and cold environments.

However, if the coat is severely matted diplomatically advise owners that a potential option is to reduce the overall coat length via clipper and comb attachment, making it easier for daily maintenance grooming.

Removal of double coat could be considered in the following scenarios: -

- Dog has skin infection and requires regular topical application of treatment
- Lifestyle of dog
- Badly neglect coat, pelted/felted
- Geriatric, may be incontinent or will not tolerate being groomed
- Behavioural will not tolerate being groomed
- Under veterinary instruction.

14.2 Hygiene Clipping

The clipping of the belly, groin and armpits to remove excess matt's and tangles is done using a fine blade taking care to avoid close clipper rash and heat burns from overheated ceramic blades. Keep skin taught to avoid skin nicks.

14.3 Thinning

Use thinning scissors to reduce the weight of the coat or blend between clipper lines and furnishings.

Thinning can be used on all coats to blend clipped areas into longer areas, is also used to reduce weight on double coated breeds as well as encouraging a natural look on long haired breeds.

Thinning scissors are also used on certain breeds (e.g. Spaniels) to achieve a natural look without damaging texture or colour of the coat.

14.4 Scissoring

There is a variety of different scissors available, all have their own general use;

- General straight scissors, typically used on dirty pre-finished coats prior to bathing and drying. These scissors can be used on all coat types.
- Finishing Scissors are used on clean/ dry coats ready for styling, particularly wool coats in a good condition. Finishing scissors give a more precise/ defined cut.

Tel: 01283 703043 Email: liza@heavenlyz.com

- Feet Scissors, usually small for cutting around feet pads and other anatomically intricate areas (e.g. ears)
- Curved Scissors create a more rounded shape

Scissoring is done to shape the coat; reduce the length of the coat; but also used under the pads and feet and on the furnishings.

Scissoring is typically used on long-haired breeds or wool coats (e.g. Poodles and Bichons).

14.5 Hand-Stripping

Hand-stripping can be used for the removal of dead coat and can be carried out on both wire and silky gundog type coats. Hand-stripping keeps the texture and colour of the coat for these specific coat types. Scissoring and clipping can be used for wire/ silk coats, but this will change the texture and colour (if hand-stripping is used repeatedly, this can permanently change texture and colour of the coat for these specific coat types.

However, hand-stripping is a highly manual, time consuming and therefore expensive process and not all pets have the correct types of coat for the procedure to be successful.

As stated, Handstripping is time-consuming. For the purposes of minimising stress to animals, Heavenlyz recommends that professional commercial groomers agree with the customer up front to simulate Handstripping by using a variety of tools. Doing so speeds up the process and makes the process more tolerable for companion dogs. The following tools are all acceptable in the commercial hand strip environment: -

- Coat kings
- Stripping Knives
- Stripping stone
- Finger thimble or condom
- Chalk
- Thinning scissors to blend and tidy face and feet

The method of commercial Handstripping will rarely cause reddening of the skin as we are mainly removing dead hair when stripping.

However, where Handstripping remains the only course of action, consider the following.

It is debatable whether to bath a wire or silk coat. Once bathed, wire or silk coat skin pores are then opened and can become irritated by both shampoo but also if then subsequently Handstripped. Most clients though, do prefer their dogs to be bathed. To bathe or not to bathe comes down to the individual dog, the owner and the salon preferred policy. Further, bathing can be done before or after Handstripping. Heavenlyz recommends that, if Handstripping is required, then it is carried out prior to bathing.

If bathing is carried out before Handstripping, then there is risk of skin irritability for reasons discussed above.

Handstripping, if carried out before bathing, is easier, because the dirty coat provides more grip to the groomers fingers.

If Handstripping is carried out after bathing and the dog shows signs of irritability, contact the owner to discuss.

Heavenlyz suggests that, if a wire/ silk coated dog owner is insistent that the dog is to be bathed and then hand stripped, explain the possible risk of bathing before hand-stripping. If the owner remains insistent, then obtain written consent, giving permission to bathe and then hand strip.

Tel: 01283 703043 Email: liza@heavenlyz.com

15 The Grooming Process

The following summarises the processes that should be considered when planning a groom: -

1. Check dog in and create/ update records
2. Carry out a health check
3. Plan your groom
4. Comb through/ rough clip
5. Hygiene clip
6. Pre-Bathe Blast
7. Feet & Nails
8. Bathe
9. Dry
10. Groom
11. Nails
12. Bows & Colognes
13. Check dog out

The following sections explore the parts of this process in more detail.

15.1 Check dog in and create/ update records

Observe the following guidelines when the dog first arrives at the salon: -

- Greet Client – maintain eye contact, smile and be polite
- Confirm the existence of the appointment and grooming requirements
- Carry out an initial health and coat/ temperament check (examine pet as it enters the salon, discuss any problems with the owner and record).
- If you notice parasitic organisms, sores or bald patches or other skin complaints: -
    - Consider whether salon policy allows the groom to go ahead
    - Check with owner/ supervisor before proceeding in case: -
        - The pet is suffering from disease (n.b. a disease that may be contagious to humans)
        - The pet is infested with parasitic organisms (in which case you should consider salon policy as well as check whether the owner has already treated the pet with anti-parasitic products (If they have and you repeat this process, it could lead to overdose)
- After the initial health check, remember to keep monitoring the dog throughout the remaining check-in process
- Confirm styling preference with owner, make sure all consent forms/ disclaimers signed (e.g. shaving matted coat etc.)
- Update the record card or fill in a new card for the new client. All salons should have a record system (paper or computerised) in place. The following mandatory information should be collected/ confirmed/ recorded: -
    - Owners name, address and contact telephone number
    - Owner named Veterinary Surgeon, Address and contact telephone number
    - Dogs Name
    - Dogs Breed
    - Dog DOB
    - Coat Colour
    - Dog Gender
    - Dog Vaccination History
    - Dog's Known Medical Conditions
    - Confirmed microchip in place – record microchip number
- Ensure you have signed authority for vet treatment, any necessary disclaimer, emergency contact number and owners' vets name on the record card.
- Obtain any necessary client consents (e.g. full clip off)

Tel: 01283 703043 Email: liza@heavenlyz.com

- Quote collection time and price before owner leaves
- Confirm who is authorised to collect the dog and, if necessary, what identification they will need bring to confirm authorisation (consider risks to your business, the dog and the client where it may not be the client who is collecting the dog)
- Take payment upfront if salon policy requires this
- Assess the dog's temperament after the owner leaves – consider appropriate use of an assistant, a muzzle or other restraint equipment

15.2 Carry out a health check

The health check is an important part of the process and enables the groomer to familiarise (or re-familiarise) themselves with the animal. Use the following process as guidance: -

- Check the dogs' records for information and advice on temperament, health concerns and shampoo preferences.
- Wash hands
- Put on PPE (e.g. grooming overall, apron) - gloves may be required if dog has a known skin disorder or Zoonotic condition (e.g. Ringworm)
- Assess temperament – consider use of an assistant/ muzzle/ other equipment.
- Confirm table and equipment required to conduct the examination are clean and ready
- Approach pet in a confident, non-threatening manner – avoid direct eye contact.
- Remove pet from kennel, using a slip lead
- Move pet at a suitable speed and keep under control
- Observe the movement of the pet, does it have any problems? (e.g. limping, etc.).
- Place the pet on the grooming table using correct lifting technique
- Be ready to record and report all findings
- Always start with examining the clean areas first (i.e. front end, eyes, nose, ears then mouth), slowly and methodically working towards the rear areas including anus and genitalia: -
    - Check eyes are clean and clear
    - Check the nose is clean and moist and that the nose skin is in good condition with no cracking or thickening
    - Check the ears are clean, free from odour, wax, redness, discharge or excessive hair. If the ears are very dirty, then clean them prior to bathing. This is done to prevent soiling the coat with ear cleansing products after the bathing and drying process.
    - Check the mouth (N.b. some dogs, notably the elderly, may have sore teeth and mouths and may not like you working around this area): -
        - In puppies, check teeth for retained puppy teeth
        - Check for sore red gums (Gingivitis), drooling and foul odour
    - Check the coat, skin and tail for signs of parasites, bald patches, cuts, sores, lumps, etc.
    - Check the body for abnormal lumps and bumps, warts etc.
    - Check the nails - do they need trimming?
    - Check the feet and pads - are there any cuts, sores? Are there matt's and tangles in between the pads or over grown nails
    - Check the genital area - is it free from discharge? Is a bitch in season? Are there any lumps/ swelling?
    - Confirm status of testicles in male dogs (Monorchid or Cryptorchid)
    - Check the anal area - is there any swelling, discharge, redness or dried in faeces?

Tel: 01283 703043 Email: liza@heavenlyz.com

- Part the coat if you notice any black dirt (this could be a sign of fleas). If evidence of fleas is discovered, consider whether salon policy allows the groom to proceed and take the following precautions to prevent contagion in other pets: -
  - Keep the dog away from other dogs
  - Prepare to sweep up hair during the groom
  - Prepare to clean and sterilise the table and equipment after the groom
  - Prepare to seal all rubbish bags after the groom (n.b. fleas can jump)
  - REMEMBER TO CHECK whether the owner has already treated the pet with anti-parasitic products (If they have and you repeat this process, it could lead to overdose)
  - If you cannot contact the owner and the salon policy is for the groom to go ahead, use a natural insect repellent and comb flea and eggs out of coat.
  - Prepare, on collection, to advise owners to treat other pets, house, car, etc. and advise them to worm the pet (because fleas are an intermediate host for tapeworm).

15.3 Plan your groom

For best results, consider all the information available and get an understanding of the steps you will take BEFORE taking those steps.

There are decisions to be made throughout the groom, some of which support the plan and some of which will require a change of plan. Understanding the following sections will allow you to identify the decisions to be made and will support proper planning.

15.4 Rough/ Pre-clip

If rough clipping is required due to matted coat, then prior to bathing: -

- Check the equipment is safe
- Check clipper leads for any breaks
- Check blades prior to use that they do not have any teeth missing which could cut the dog
- Clip the pet into the style required by the owner/ breed or, if in the interest of the dog's welfare and you hold the owner's consent, carry out full coat removal, including all furnishings (note that this must be done avoiding clipper alopecia and clipper lines).
- Take care blades do not get hot on a dirty, matted coat and become clogged.
- Change blades regularly (rotate the blades or have separate blades used only to rough clip; keep blades used on clean coats separate from those used on dirty coats)
- Excess hair may also be removed from the feet by scissoring

15.5 Hygiene Clip

This is normally done on all coat types except double coat and smooth coats as well as where the owner advises against hair removal.

If the coat is matted, it is recommended that this is carried out before the bathing process. If the coat is not matted, this part of the process can be done after the bathing process.

This part of the process includes removal of excess hair from the belly, groin and armpits.

15.6 Pre-Bathe Blast

On the following types of dogs, a pre-bathe blast (using a high velocity blaster) may be helpful: -

- **Double coated breeds** with a heavily compacted undercoat can be blasted to loosen the hair
- **Dense coated breeds** (e.g. Samoyeds/ Pomeranians/ Newfoundland's) can be blasted until the hair lifts and the skin can be seen.

Tel: 01283 703043 Email: liza@heavenlyz.com

15.7 Feet & Nails

In certain cases, grooming the feet and nails before bathing should be considered.

If there are bad matts found in the pads these may be clipped out with a fine blade (no. 10/ 15/ 30 blade or scissor) prior to bathing.

Nails are usually trimmed after bathing. This is because the bathing process frequently softens the nail making it easier to shorten with clippers. For further information regards nails, see 15.11 below.

The nails of white or light coated dogs may be shortened before or during the bathe in case of accidental trimming of the quick (as well as avoiding a cut nail bleeding over white/ light coats).

15.8 Bathe

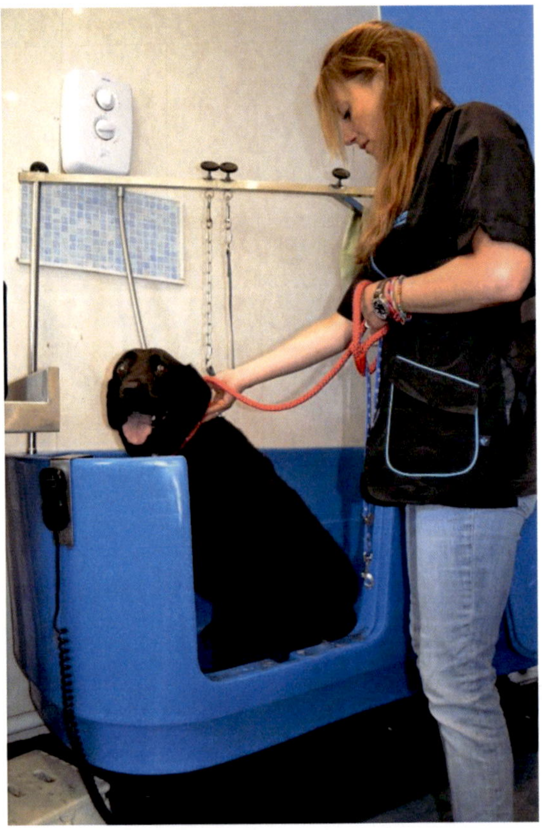

Dogs do not necessarily need to be bathed before the hair length is modified. However, for best results and where coat circumstances allow, a bathe is recommended. Dogs who come into the salon wet or dirty are highly likely to need bathing prior to grooming.

15.8.1 Assess for the correct time to bathe

Is it best to bathe before or after clipping and styling? Well, a clean coat brushes out faster and easier than a dirty coat so, if water can penetrate the fur, wash the dog first. However, bathing of a felted or matted coat prior to combing or clipping coat risks the following problems: -

- You would not be able clean the skin due to the felted matting
- You would not be able to rinse all the shampoo out of the coat as the matting would hold it
- Drying the coat after bathing would cause the coat to shrink and the matts to tighten.

So, there are exceptions – if there are areas of severe matting/ felting and you are trying to save the coat, consider the following pre-bathe: -

- brushing and breaking open the matts prior to bathing.
- rough clip

15.8.2 Pre-Bathe brush out routine

Prior to bathing, a brush out routine, as follows, is recommended: -

1. Check the equipment prior to use
2. Check the grooming area is safe and clean for use
3. Start at the bottom of the foot on the back leg and brush the hair, in layers from the skin outwards
4. Remember to do the same for the inside of the opposite leg that you are working on and to check under the armpits
5. Work forwards from the back legs towards the front legs up into the body and then into the face and ears.
6. Use slicker brush, Les Pooch/ Activet® brushes to break out the coat
7. A matt breaker or de-matting comb can be used to aid breaking open knots or tangle, thinning scissors may also be used to thin through the mats then brush and comb out until the comb passes through the coat.
8. Ensure all matts are broken open so water can penetrate the skin
9. The bathing and blasting will help to further break open and clean the coat making it easier to brush and de-matt after bathing.

Tel: 01283 703043 Email: liza@heavenlyz.com

15.8.3 Shampoos

Bathing can be done as often as the client requests, providing that a good quality shampoo is used to restore the coats' natural oils. There are 5 main types of Shampoo: -

- **Cleansing** – These contain strong substances that act against dirt and grease
- **Mild** – Contains mild substances to remove dirt and grease, leaves some of the coats natural oils, works well for dogs with sensitive skin.
- **Insecticidal** – These kill parasites
- **Medicated** – These contain mild anti-bacterial products
- **Veterinary** – Prescription shampoo

Employ the following precautions to ensure safe use of shampoo: -

- Disposal gloves and any other PPE should be worn where recommended by manufacturer
- Check the shampoo is for the pet prescribed
- Read and follow the instructions.
- Prevent the dog from licking shampoo (consider use of an Elizabethan collar)

Consider that the removal of stubborn substances, such as oil or tar, can be eased by emulsifying with a tiny amount of diluted washing up liquid. Apply the diluted washing up liquid to the affected area only, leave for five to ten minutes, then shampoo as normal. **Caution:** use diluted washing up liquid only – washing up liquid can strip the coat of its natural oils – and make sure that you rinse thoroughly.

15.8.4 The Bathing Process

When bathing work to a routine: -

- Deploy wet floor warning boards
- Collect all equipment and tools
- Consider use of a Happy Hoodie – this can significantly help, especially in the prevention of head shaking
- Prepare shampoo, ensure manufacturer's dilution instructions are followed correctly
- Prepare restraining aids
- Ensure the bath is safe, clean and ready to use.
- Prepare bath height
- Ensure bath at correct height for groomer and dog with appropriate restraints
- Where necessary, seek restraint assistance for young, ill or large breeds
- Check the water temperature on the inside of your wrist to make sure it is at body temperature (prepare to repeat this periodically during the bath, especially immediately after periods where the shower head has not been held)
- Collect the dog, move dog to and into the bath, employing best practice throughout
- Make sure the dog is secure in the bath (use a non-slip mat in bottom of bath)
- Note that some dogs may try to bite the shower head or the water.

Tel: 01283 703043 Email: liza@heavenlyz.com

- Take special care that small dogs and short nosed breeds do not inhale water (this increases risk of "dry drowning").

- Wet the dog, keep shower head close to body, starting behind shoulders and working back over the body, down the legs and tail.
- Leave the head until last. This will help reduce the chance of the dog shaking to remove water from itself. It will also help give the dog time to get used the water (especially useful with a first-time bather or nervous dog).
- Work the water into the coat until it is completely saturated
- Avoid water entering ears and nose
- Avoid emptying anal glands – Heavenlyz recommends that this is an activity that should be carried out by a veterinary professional only. If working correctly, dogs' anal glands self-empty as a motion is passed. If there is a problem, then this should be diagnosed by a veterinary surgeon under the Veterinary Surgeons' Act 1966 and it is the veterinary surgeon who alone should advise.
- Apply the correctly diluted shampoo using a sponge to create a lather
- Always start shampooing at the back of the dog (this gives you more time to assess temperament)
- Begin to apply shampoo to the tail and anal area, dried on faeces etc. working down both back legs and finishing at hind feet
- Shampoo body and undercarriage, front legs, shoulders, chest.
- Work towards the head
- Shampoo the head last and rinse it first so that risk of soap getting into the dogs' eyes is reduced

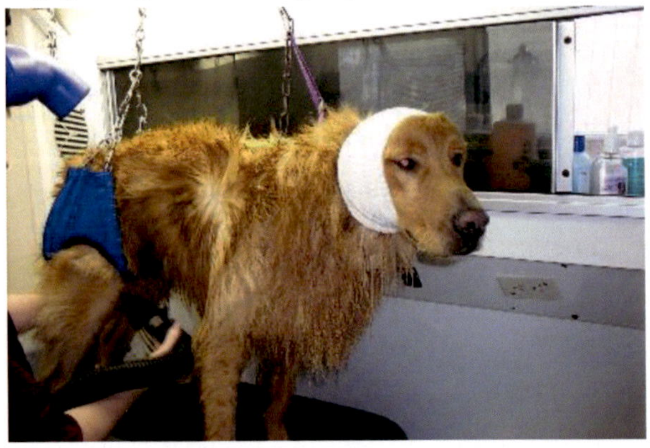

- Finally (and carefully) ensure that the head is wet and apply the shampoo (avoiding eyes, ears, mouth and nose)
- Rinse the dog head to tail, use your hands to push the suds and water through and out of the coat
- To prevent head shaking a Happy Hoodie can be used throughout the bathing and drying process. The Happy Hoodie is a soft, expandable, gentle compression fabric band that relieves anxiety and calms dogs during what they feel to be a stressful situation such as using a blaster. It has a calming, almost swaddling, effect on dogs. It can also be used on dry coats to prevent head shaking, especially after heavy coat removal from ear. This would be done to prevent head shaking and risk of aural haematoma.
- **A second shampoo** is usual for greasy or dirty coats. It may also be salon policy that all dogs receive a second shampoo – in which case, repeat the shampooing process above
- Rinse thoroughly, ensuring coat is clean and **'squeaky'** (this is a term used by groomers - if all shampoo residue has been removed, then when the water is pushed through the coat by hand, it will make a squeaking noise)
- Apply conditioner as required or as is salon policy, rinsing if the conditioner has been necessary
- Rinse and squeeze out excess water with your hands or absorbent towel
- Wire coats if the coat is to be hand-stripped all the stripping should be done prior to bathing. Bathing prior to hand-stripping would soften the coat making it harder to strip.

Tel: 01283 703043 Email: liza@heavenlyz.com

15.9 Dry

Application of correct drying equipment, processes and techniques will help remove knots and tangles, remove dead undercoat and straighten the coat ready for trimming and the desired finish.

15.9.1 Drying Equipment

15.9.1.1 Towel

The towel and its use in towel drying is a critical part of the drying process for most dogs. By thoroughly squeezing out excess water by hand then applying an absorbent cloth or towel to proper extraction the water will reduce your drying time drastically whilst saving on electricity bills, help reduce carbon footprint and speed up the process. There are many commercially available types of towels that can be used: -

- Regular bath towels
- Microfibre towels
- Moisture magnets
- Chamois
- Absorber

Care for the young and old dogs consider the use of a warm towel can make the dog more comfortable, so if possible, use one that is warmed up.

If using an absorbent cloth type towel, then a warmer is not an option. The Moisture magnets and Absorber type towels work better when they are wet to begin with. Simply wring them out and they are ready to go back to work again

15.9.1.2 Blaster

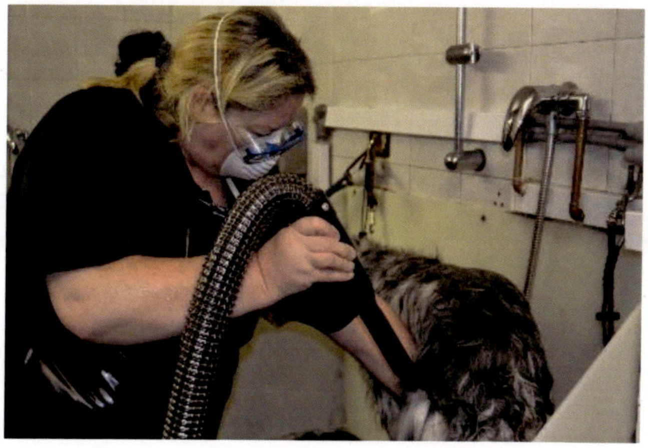

The blaster allows for high velocity air drying and helps to: -

- reduce drying time
- loosen compacted dead hair, matt's and tangles
- reduce brushing time
- mitigate trauma to a dog's skin (straightening the hair without a lot of brushing or heavy heat reduces the risk of brush burn and heat stress/stroke)

Blasting also helps open dense coats in preparation to blow drying, it can help reduce drying time.

15.9.1.3 Cabinet/ Cage Dryer

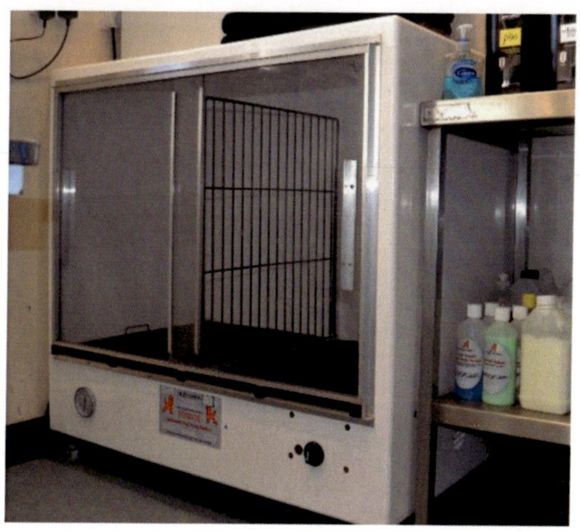

A cabinet or cage dryer is used mainly for straight coated breeds, but not for wool coats where a straight fluff finish is required. A gentle airflow helps dry the coat whilst the dog sits securely in an enclosed cabinet.

Caution: constantly observe Dogs when using the cabinet dryer for signs of over-heating or distress.

Warning: -

- Short nosed breeds should not be placed in the Cabinet dryer as it could impair their ability to breathe and cause respiratory distress.
- Dense coats should also not be placed in the cabinet dryer as it could lead to the dog overheating.

15.9.1.4 Stand Dryer

A Stand Dryer/ Fluff Dryer allows the groomer to have two hands free for brushing the dog during the drying process. This situation is also known as straight drying. It is ideal when removing matts and allows the groomer to achieve a straight finish on the coat.

Caution Care should be taken not to cause brush burns from constant brushing in the same area.

15.9.2 Coat considerations

Different coat types require different tools and drying methods: -

Tel: 01283 703043 Email: liza@heavenlyz.com

- Smooth coats can be dried in a cabinet/ cage dryer and finished off with a stand dryer (as well as a slicker on thicker coats). To avoid skin irritation, a hand glove can be used to dry very smooth coat breeds with little hair.
- Double coats need to be dried using a stand dryer and a slicker to break open the coat. A de-matting rake and/ or undercoat rake can be used to remove excess dead hair. If there are bad matts the double-sided thinners can be used to thin through the matts, followed by a brush and comb out. A Moult Master may be used to remove dead coat and a Coat Controller may also be used to thin the coat.
- Show or Silky coats need to be dried straight using a pin brush and, if the coat is matted, a comb. A Matt Breaker or matt zapper can be used to remove matts. Avoid slicker use as this can break the coat.
- If a gundog coat is to be stripped and salon policy allows, a "Coat King" may be used along the dog's back whilst drying to remove dead hair. The "Coat King" has its place in commercial grooming but is considered by some as an inappropriate tool as it cuts the topcoat as well as removing dead undercoat. A slicker comb can then be used on all the furnishings to straighten.
- Wool coats need to be dried straight to aid scissoring (use the stand dryer).

15.9.3 Drying Method

Caution: -

- ensure area and the equipment for drying pet is safe, clean and ready to use
- remember to dry your hands before using electrical equipment and to wear appropriate PPE.

Employ an appropriate drying methodology: -

- Towel dry – towel drying may sound simple, but for a commercial groomer there are key steps to drying efficiently with a towel. Begin by squeezing excess water out of the coat with your hands while still in the tub. Then, using a squeezing motion again, absorb as much water as you can with your towel. Change towels as they get wet to minimise time spent/ coat rubbing, especially with long hair coats (this creates tangles). **NEVER** re-use towels from one dog to another as this could lead to potential cross contamination. Always use a clean towel on each dog and wash between uses.
- Blaster dry – begin the drying process by removing excess water and dead hair. Make sure that long coats are blasted downwards with the air jet close to the skin – this will reduce tangling the coat. Do not Blast in a circular movement as it will tangle the coat and do not blast around or near the dog's eyes, ears and genital areas.
- Hands free stand dry - brush the coat to separate the coat removing dead undercoat, knots and tangle Best results are when the coat is dried using a cabinet then finished with a stand dryer. Section the coat and work in a methodical order. Brushing the coat from root to tip will create a straight finish to the coat especially desirable for wool coats. Be careful not to brush too much in the one spot as this may cause brush burn. Work in sections. Start at the bottom of the back leg and work up, then do the inside of the opposite legs and work forward where you repeat the process on the front legs. Leave the head until last.

15.10 Grooming

Learning to groom safely is best carried out under the instructions of a professional. For instructions regards the use of plucking, stripping, clipping and scissoring techniques Heavenlyz recommends the outstanding practical training offered by any one of the centres listed on the Heavenlyz website under training schools...

http://www.heavenlyz.com/training-schools/

15.11 Nails

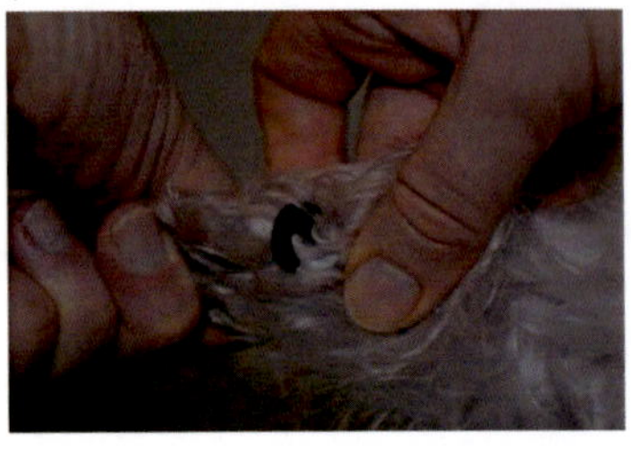

Caution: the nail has a blood vessel within, called the "Quick". If you clip the nails too short, then the quick will be cut, the nail will bleed, and this will cause pain and distress to the dog.

The following process can be used as nail clipping guidance: -

- Restrain the Dog; you may require an assistant to help restrain and reassure.
- Examine each foot and individual nails; look for signs of inflammation especially around the nail bed.

Tel: 01283 703043 Email: liza@heavenlyz.com

- Select the appropriate size nail clippers
- The clipping action will exert a rotating force on the nail. Hold the nail firmly between your fingers and thumb; this will help prevent the nail rotating within the nail bed, with the pressure of the clipping action.
- Locate the nails Quick
- Cut below the Quick (i.e. towards the tip of the nail), removing the pointed tip of the nail
- Smooth any rough edges with a nail file if required

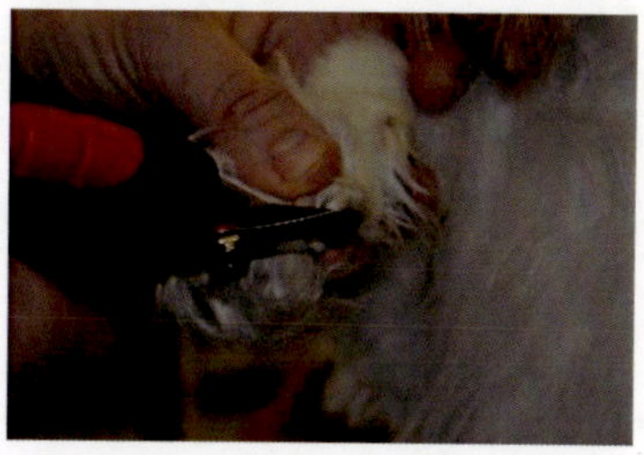

Have a Coagulant agent at hand to stop any bleeding in case the Quick is accidentally cut.

If nails are discovered to be overgrown or embedded into the pad, it is advisable to alleviate pressure by cutting the nail in two. This must be done avoiding the quick, using plier type nail clippers. However, do not remove the embedded nail. Instead, advise the owner to visit the veterinary surgeon as soon as possible (today is recommended), such that a qualified veterinary professional can remove and provide appropriate wound management advice.

15.12 Bows and Colognes

Consider going a little bit further and stand out from your competitors. Usually, most clients appreciate your finishing efforts. However, a word of caution, document your clients' preferences and get agreement beforehand. Ensure that the client has agreed to the finishing touches you might apply before you hand back a dog whose appearance may not suit its, or its owners, lifestyle.

Caution: attach bows to dog's collar or lead. Do not attach bows direct to the dog's coat as this may cause damage/pain.

Colognes are also a very personal choice. If you are going to use cologne, ensure that the dog does not have any skin allergies which may worsen with the application of the cologne.

15.13 Check Out for the Dog

To prepare the dog for going home, transfer the dog to the holding area awaiting collection. Ensure the 5 animal needs are still observed. On client arrival, the following process is recommended to ensure that the client focusses on what you have to report/ next steps that you will need to take: -

- Meet the client (or the representative of the client) in a friendly manner and confirm their identity
- Discuss the grooming services undertaken
- Alert the owner to any issues or concern/ health problems detected
- Take payment
- Encourage arrangement of next appointment
- [Optional] client to sign a check out form, demonstrating that the dog has been handed back in an agreed state. This is especially recommended where it is not the dog's owner who arrived with and/ or collected the dog
- Hand the dog back to the (representative of the) client

Tel: 01283 703043 Email: liza@heavenlyz.com

16 Animal Health

To recognise signs of ill health, it is first essential to be familiar with vital signs/ signs of good health.

16.1 Normal health check values

Temperature	38.3-38.7c 100.9-101.7f	Recommend use of a (rectal) professional thermometer
Pulse	60-160 beats per minute	The smaller the dog, the faster the pulse
Respiratory Rate	10-30 breaths a minute	The smaller the dog, the faster the respiratory rate
Capillary Refill Time	1-2 seconds	Recommended to press gently on the gum to measure this

16.2 Method of measuring Temperature

The usual method of for taking the temperature is using the rectal route. Temperature can be taken with a digital electronic thermometer that is lubricated with a water-soluble or petroleum gel gently inserted 1-2 cm into the rectum.

16.3 Method of measuring pulse

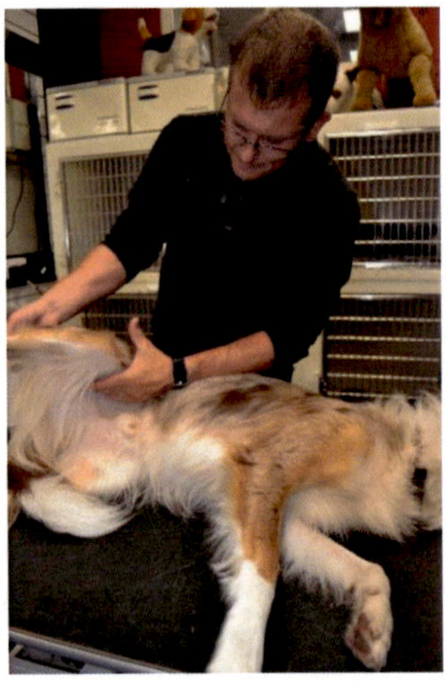

The pulse of a dog can be felt anywhere an artery runs near to the body surface – each pulse corresponds to a contraction (beat) of the heart. The recommended point of pulse monitoring is the Femoral artery, which lies high up along the inside of the back leg, between two large muscles where the leg joins the body. To take the pulse: -

- Restrain the dog effectively, with the use of an assistant if possible
- Use gentle restraint – as little as needed
- Locate the artery and count the pulses felt for one minute to get the number of beats per minute (bpm)
- Or count for 30 seconds and multiply by 2 for bpm
- Or count for 20 seconds and multiply by 3 for bpm
- Or count for 15 seconds and multiply by 4 for bpm, etc...

16.4 Method of measuring respiratory rate

To assess respiration, stand above or behind the dog or place your hands gently on either side of the chest and observe/ feel the chest and/or abdomen moving with each breath

- Count the breaths in or out (not both) for one minute to get the number of breaths per minute (bpm)
- Or count for 30 seconds and multiply by 2 for bpm, etc.

16.5 Method of measuring capillary refill time

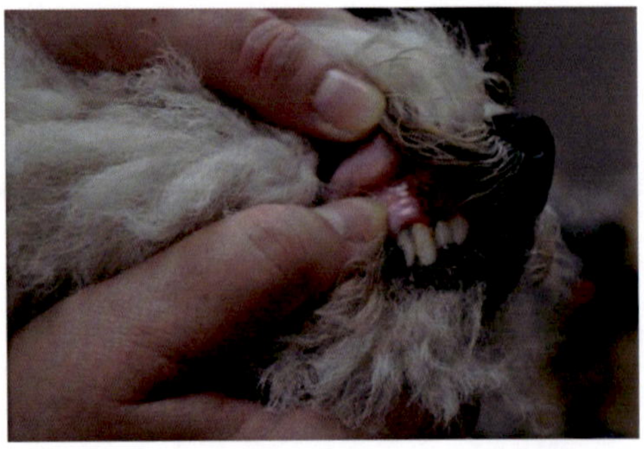

Mucous membrane (MM) colour and Capillary refill time (CRT)

- The gums of a healthy animal are usually moist and have a salmon pink colour
- When gently pressed with the thumb, the colour blanches to white
- The normal colour should return within 2 seconds

Tel: 01283 703043 Email: liza@heavenlyz.com

- A failure to do so could indicate haemorrhage, shock or dehydration
- MMs that are very pale pink, very dark red, white, yellow or blue are abnormal
- Dry or sticky gums may indicate dehydration
- Bruising may be evident on MMs and may indicate a bleeding problem

16.6 Normal appearance of the dog

- Clear bright eyes
- Alert expression
- Pink mucous membranes
- Clean and odour free ears
- Shiny coat
- Good appetite
- Free limb movement
- Firm brown faeces (2-3 times a day)
- Clear yellow urine (3-4 times a day)

16.7 Health maintenance

Remember prevention is much better than cure. We can put specific measures in place to promote wellbeing, maintain and help prevent deterioration of dog's health. These measures include: -

- Vaccination
- Worming
- Neutering
- Dental care
- Regular health checks
- Adequate exercise
- Grooming

16.8 Nutritional considerations

It's commonly known that to maintain a dog's optimum health a balanced diet is required. A balanced diet consists of nutrients found in food essential for the dog's body to maintain normal function. There are 6 key nutrients: -

- Water
- Carbohydrates
- Fat
- Protein
- Minerals
- Vitamins

Feeding amounts should be appropriate to the dog's individual needs and will vary according to: -

- Life stage
- Age
- Size and breed
- Health status
- Dogs activity levels
- Lifestyle and purpose

16.9 Water

As Groomers the main nutrient that will concern us is water. Water is vital to prevent dehydration, which could lead to the more serious risk of becoming over heated. It is vital that all dogs have access to fresh water throughout the grooming process. It is particularly important to observe this throughout the drying process or when a dog has a known condition such as diabetes or is on medication which may affect water intake.

Knowing how to calculate the required daily amount of water for an individual dog is a requirement of many qualification examinations.

It is best to give dog's water little and often – doing so will also help you monitor how much water they need. A dog's daily water intake depends on several factors such as: -

- Size: On average, a healthy dog may require between 50ML and 100ML water per KG bodyweight.
- Food: A healthy diet is as important as water. The type of eaten by a dog affects their water intake (e.g. dogs that eat only dry food will need more water than those that eat canned food). Avoid ingredients that can artificially increase your dog's thirst (e.g. sodium/ salt)
- Age: All dogs should be monitored, Puppies need to be closely monitored. Senior dogs tend to naturally monitor themselves. Dogs of any age group may need encouragement to drink.
- Exercise: take water along on any exercise outing with your dog. The bottles that have the drop-down cup work well. After exercise, monitor amount dog drinks, little and often is good and this helps to prevent risk of bloat.
- Weather: Summer means more panting which means an increase in water intake.

Tel: 01283 703043 Email: liza@heavenlyz.com

- Medications: Some drugs increase a dog's thirst. Check with your vet to see if you need to decrease or increase your dog's water intake while taking new medication
- There is no feasible circumstance in which it is acceptable to give a dog alcohol.

16.10 Checking for dehydration in dogs

To look for dehydration in dogs, gently pinch a piece of skin at the back of your dog's neck. Stretch it out, then let it go. A properly hydrated dog's skin will snap quickly back into place, while the skin of a dehydrated dog will return slowly and form a "**tent**" in the process. You can also check your dog's gums for dehydration - wet, slippery gums are healthy. Dull, sticky gums suggest dehydration.

Insuring that the dogs in your care maintain proper hydration during their stay is part of your duty of care as a groomer.

Dogs in the salon tend to drink less than they should and have increased risk of becoming dehydrated. Dogs more at risk of dehydration are the young and old, dogs with a known disease or ailment and those on medication that is likely to increase thirst.

Conversely, drinking too much can also be problematic. To avoid the risk of consuming large amount of water in one go whilst staying at the salon, the 'Over-Drinkers' could be given ice cubes to lick.

16.11 Provision of clean water

To help ensure that the water supply dogs in your care is clean, you can do one simple action – **clean up after the dog**. Water bowls with dirty and stagnant water left outside is unacceptable. Water vessels should be properly washed/ disinfected between dogs, this must occur at least daily.

Topping up water in a dirty bowl will contribute to the risk of ill health. Consider especially Leptospirosis – this is spread by rodents, who may be apparent outside your premises during closing hours, urinating in and around bowls. This carries a high risk of water contamination and, if this occurs, will infect the dogs who attend the salon on the next day.

The part of the animal welfare act that lists the 5 animal needs, includes the right to protection from disease.

Water bowls should be individual, cleaned daily and put down fresh every morning. Most salons now operate a system where dogs are offered water between each treatment or who are left with a small amount in a bowl attached to their individual holding unit.

Having spent several hours 'fluff' drying and styling a wool coat, any mess incurred by drinking water could be viewed as counterproductive or frustrating. However, our prime concern is the health and well-being of animals in our care and water must be offered at regular intervals until the dog leaves the salon.

16.12 Food

It is important that dogs in the salon are not fed unless instructed by the owner, in case we interfere with the dog's diet. Many dogs suffer from food intolerances which would be aggravated if we fed an unknown food source. Groomers are only asked to feed a dog on a few occasions, at the owner's request, usually for the following situations: -

- Puppy
- Pregnant or lactating bitch
- Animal on medication and food is required when medicating
- Metabolic disorder such as diabetes

Groomers should encourage dog owners to seek advice from their veterinary surgeon on all health matters including dietary matters. A basic understanding of nutritional requirements is required.

16.12.1 Growing dogs

Puppies receive their nutrients from feeding on their mother's milk. As a general guide, from 3-4 weeks of age puppies can start to be prepared for weaning by introducing a "mushy food" based diet in addition to their mother's milk.

At 6 weeks of age puppies are usually weaned away from mother's milk. Slight underfeed is preferred to overfeed, as conditions such as Hip Dysplasia have been shown to be aggravated by incorrect diet during the growth stage of development.

Meals should be divided into 3-4 meals and fed at set intervals throughout the day allowing time to eat, usually 20-30 minutes may be required.

Tel: 01283 703043 Email: liza@heavenlyz.com

Please seek veterinary advice on feeding a growing dog.

16.12.2 Active Dogs

Working dogs such as police, herding and assistant dogs are exposed to a variety of stressful situations and require higher calories to enable them to perform throughout the day and maintain stamina and endurance.

16.12.3 Obesity

A healthy weight can be determined by feeling the ribcage – ribs should be easily felt with a little flesh between fingers when you pinch the skin. The following attributes promote obesity in dogs: -

- Female
- Neutered
- Old age
- Breed predisposition (e.g. Labrador)
- Sedentary lifestyle
- Home-made diets that are unhealthy
- Excessive treating
- Over feeding

To reduce body weight, the best advice is to feed an energy restricted, low fat and high in fibre diet divided into small meals and given throughout the day.

In association with this, daily exercise should be increased. Doing this will prevent boredom.

Please seek veterinary advice when planning a restricted calorie diet for an overweight dog.

16.12.4 Older dogs

The aim for the care of an older dog is to improve quality of life by maintain optimum health. The main requirements and consideration for feeding an older dog are as follows: -

- Reduce amount fed if the dog is not as active as previously.
- Feed high quality protein but not so much as too exceed the adult dog protein requirements. Feeding too much protein may lead to deteriorative renal disease.
- Increasing fibre may promote constipation
- Food is to be highly palatable and easily digestible
- Allow dog to freely exercise at their own pace to reduce risk of obesity

16.12.5 Food intolerance

It is difficult to identify individual food ingredients which cause intolerance. Common ingredients such as protein found in beef or milk, carbohydrate found in wheat and lactose and food additives such as colourings and preservatives are all known to cause intolerances.

In dogs, dietary intolerance most commonly affects the skin and digestive system. Amongst other debilitating conditions, this can cause eczema, itchy skin, dermatitis, otitis (ear inflammation), diarrhoea, vomiting, abdominal discomfort and colitis.

Ingredient elimination trials are the only reliable method to determine possible cause of intolerance. If symptoms improve with an ingredient eliminated from the dog's diet, then that could be considered a probable cause. The completion of a food diary is mandatory for a trial to be of success. Ensure that all food eaten is written down and tracked.

Also ensure that all persons responsible for the dog's care are aware of the strict diet for a successful elimination to take place. Be aware that dietary intolerance usually improves within a few days whereas skin irritations may take 3-4 weeks before an improvement is seen. It is advisable to seek veterinary advice when conducting food trials.

16.12.6 Change in Diet

To avoid diarrhoea or other gastric problems, it is recommended that a change in diet is introduced over a period of days. Though it is recommended to seek the advice of a veterinary surgeon first, the following general rule applies: -

- Day one ¼ of the new diet is added to ¾ usual foods
- Day two ½ new diet to ½ usual food
- Day three ¾ new diet and ¼ original diet

Tel: 01283 703043 Email: liza@heavenlyz.com

- Day four new diet only

Observe faeces passed daily to ensure that it remains the desired consistency and frequency. A general rule is that you should be able to collect the faeces in a scoop/ bag with the faeces only leaving a slight surface residual behind and that those faeces should be firm to the touch.

16.13 Exercise Considerations

An individual dog's exercise is just that, "individual". As a rule, the dog should only be exercised to its own level of comfort. Observe the signs of fatigue and stop for a rest. Never force a dog to continue.

Adult dogs tend to be more aware of their bodies, and if they start to become hot, tired and in need of a rest, they usually slow down the pace, start falling behind, pant heavily, sit down and stop to rest.

The young are usually so preoccupied with the excitement of their exercise that they may miss signs of fatigue and over exert themselves. The following are reasons for providing exercise: -

- Prevent obesity
- Prevent boredom and associated conditions
- Socialisation
- Provide opportunity to urinate and defecate
- Improve and maintain muscles
- Improve heart and lung function

16.13.1 Types of exercise

The following are the main types of exercise: -

- **Free exercise** – allows animals to exercise at own pace, exhibit natural behaviour or personality.
- **Controlled exercise** – equipment used to restrain and control the animal
- **Fenced exercise** – a compound securely fenced, allows animal to be free but still in a controlled environment, good when training or socialising.
- **Hydrotherapy** – water-aided exercise, most appropriate for dogs with chronic degenerative joint disease. Exercise using water is excellent for obese dogs or those with a pre-existing condition. This is because their body weight is supported by water and swimming/ walking through water creates resistance helping muscle tone and development.

16.13.2 Exercise and dog's life stages

An individual dogs exercise requirement will alter throughout its life.

- **Puppies and adolescent dogs;** require short bouts of exercise, at their own pace, exercise should not be forced as their bone, muscle and ligaments are not developed and permanent damage can occur. The breed of dog will influence when they will develop and mature.
- **Mature dogs;** gradually increase the duration and intensity of exercise to maintain health during the adult life stage
- **Geriatric/ seniors;** exercise requirements will vary again dependant on the individual, health status, breed and other factors which may have an impact on exercise. Allow the dog to exercise at their own pace, providing stimulation other than exercise such as mental mind games, of which there are many commercially available or treat filled toys.

A general rule with all life stages is to maintain mental health by providing activities which stimulate. A dog will find a game of fetch in a garden as rewarding as a long walk in the country. Learn to read the dog requirements and act on their needs. Remember to adjust your daily routine to prevent boredom. Consider environmental factors such as avoiding exercise in the hottest part of the day/ ensuring the dog stays hydrated.

Tel: 01283 703043 Email: liza@heavenlyz.com

16.13.3 Specific Breed and Health considerations;

- **Dogs with pre-existing conditions** such as hip or elbow arthritis, cruciate ligament rupture in the knee, joint and spinal problems, cardiac disease and so on, should never be forced to exercise. Allow these dogs limited exercise at their own pace, which will help maintain joint flexibility and prevent boredom and weight gain**. Hydrotherapy** is a good alternative. However, advice from a veterinary surgeon before developing an exercise regime should be sought.
- **Physical appearance** of the dog will have an impact on its exercise requirements. The **brachycephalic** breeds are such an example, including breeds as the Pug, French Bulldog and Boston Terrier. All have a shortened nose and compressed faces, impairing airflow through the upper respiratory tract, making these breeds susceptible to overheating when over exercised, a life-threatening condition.
- **Obesity** in dogs can have significant health implications, causing orthopaedic, cardiac, hepatic and dermatological disease. Advise the owner that they seek advice from a veterinary surgeon to discuss dietary requirements and exercise. A basic exercise plan should be drawn up, particularly if the dog has led a sedentary lifestyle. Build exercise gradually until a moderate level is attained.
- **Deep Chested Breeds** for example Great Danes or Boxers, there is concern that exercising deep chested breeds on a full stomach can have implications associated with the condition 'Bloat' or 'Stomach/ Gastric Torsion'. This has neither been proven nor unproven, so Heavenlyz recommends not exercising an hour before or after feeding.

Research the dogs breed history and origin. This will give you an inclination of the dog's exercise requirements.

16.14 Signs of Illness in Dogs

SIGN	**POSSIBLE CAUSE**
Blue Tinged Membranes (cyanosis)	Respiratory Obstruction
Yellow tinged membranes (icterus or jaundice)	Liver Disease Leptospirosis
Pale mucous membranes (Anaemia)	Haemorrhage Anaemia Shock Circulatory Failure
Brick Red mucous membranes	Heat stress/ stroke
Constipation	Lack Exercise Dehydration Inappropriate feeding
Coughing	Inhalation chemicals Kennel Cough Infectious disease e.g. Distemper Heart or Respiratory Failure
Diarrhoea	Change Diet Endoparasites Infection/Infectious Disease

Tel: 01283 703043 Email: liza@heavenlyz.com

SIGN	POSSIBLE CAUSE
Discharge from Ear	Ear Mites Infection Foreign Body i.e. grass seed
Discharge from Eye	Distemper Kennel Cough Foreign Body
Discharge from Nose	Distemper Kennel Cough Foreign Body Respiratory Disease
High Temperature (hyperthermia)	Pain Distress Infection Heat stroke Excitement
Low Temperature (hypothermia)	Shock Circulatory collapse Impending Parturition
Rapid Pulse	Fever Exercise Pain Fear
Rapid Respiration	Exercise Heat Pain Poison
Vaginal Discharge	Normal if part of the oestrous cycle Pyometra
Vomiting	Endoparasites Foreign Body Poisoning Infectious disease
Increased frequency (polyuria) and volume of urine	Increased thirsts Disease Medication

Tel: 01283 703043 Email: liza@heavenlyz.com

SIGN	POSSIBLE CAUSE
Increased thirst (polydipsia) and consumption of water	Disease Medication Pyometra/ phantom pregnancy vomiting
Change in colour of urine and faeces (orange colour)	Disease dehydration

If at any stage of the grooming process the dog's health deteriorates stop the grooming process, call for assistance, examine the dog and seek advice from owner/ veterinary surgeon.

Tel: 01283 703043 Email: liza@heavenlyz.com

17 Common Breed Disorders

Breed Disorders are usually associated with pure bred breeds and are usually inherited from one or both parents. Certain breeds can be associated with a certain disorder. It is recommended that further reading is required to fully understand individual breed disorders. This section also covers common injuries, parasites and diseases.

17.1 Skin Disorders

The following are typical skin disorders found within the grooming salon: -

- Lick Dermatitis - a complex disorder where the dog will lick constantly at an area usually on their legs. The area becomes raw and ulcerated, usually a secondary infection occurs. It is associated with boredom; however other contributing factors can be considered such as obsessive-compulsive disorder or a disorder of the sensory nerves. **Breeds affected by Lick dermatitis** includes: - Labrador retriever, Great Dane, German Shepherd Dog and Doberman
- Fold Dermatitis - Dermatitis meaning inflammation of the skin, where excessive skin folds or wrinkles trap in moisture and rub against each other causing pyoderma, a bacterial skin infection. Usually seen on the facial folds, lips and tail area. **Breeds affected by Skin Fold Dermatitis** include; Bloodhounds, Boston Terrier (tail fold) Chinese Shar-Pei, Cocker and Springer spaniel (lip fold), English Bulldog (facial fold), Pug (facial and tail fold)
- Canine Acne - Canine acne is usually seen in young adults, acne develops on their chin. Lips and muzzle, commonly called "blackheads". **Breeds affected by Canine Acne** include; Boxers, Dobermans, English Bulldogs, Great Danes

17.2 Eye Disorders

Eye Disorders - If you suspect eye disorder, report to the owner immediately. A modification of the grooming process may be required. If you suspect the condition will deteriorate were the groom to continue, stop immediately and make the dog comfortable.

- Ectropion – where the eyelid sags or rolls out, abnormally exposing the eye, which can lead to irritation, commonly seen with breeds with exaggerated facial features where it is often a breed characteristic. **Breeds affected by Ectropion** include; Basset Hound, Boxer, Springer Spaniel, Shih Tzu.
- Entropion – where the eyelid rolls inwards onto the eye, most commonly the lower lid. This irritates the eye surface and may cause visual impairment. Commonly seen in breeds with exaggerated facial features with prominent eyes or heavy facial folds. **Breeds affected by Entropion include**; Chow Chow, Shar-Pei and Bullmastiff.
- Glaucoma (disease of the optic nerve) - defined as an increase in the intra-ocular pressure of the dog's eye (inner eye pressure). Glaucoma is common in certain dog breeds that are genetically predisposed, such as Samoyeds, Cocker Spaniels, Poodles, Chow Chows, and Siberians. Glaucoma is a condition in which pressure is placed on the eye, causing inadequate fluid drainage. If the condition becomes chronic or persists without treatment, it will eventually cause permanent damage to the optic nerve, resulting in blindness. Symptoms for Glaucoma as seen within the grooming room are typically as follows: -
    - Blinking of the eye
    - The eyeball may recede back into the head
    - Redness of the blood vessels in the whites of eyes
    - Cloudy appearance at front of the eye
    - Dilated pupil – or pupil does not respond to light
    - Vision loss
    - Enlargement eye

17.3 Musculoskeletal Disorders

17.3.1 Elbow Dysplasia

This refers to several conditions affecting the elbow, affects large breeds and usually more than often affects both front legs, the dog will show lameness and elbow pain. **Breeds affected by Elbow** Dysplasia include; Labrador retriever, Golden Retriever, Basset Hound, Chow Chow.

Tel: 01283 703043 Email: liza@heavenlyz.com

17.3.2 Hip Dysplasia

This is caused when there is a loose fit between the ball and socket joint of the hip, the ligaments that joint them together are loose and the ball joint may slide part way out of the socket. Dogs with Hip Dysplasia show pain, lame and have a weak hind end. The disorder will get worse overtime. Large to Giant breeds are mainly affected, when purchasing a dog from a breeder ask for a hip certificate of their breeding dogs, and for several generations in the past. **Breeds affected by Hip Dysplasia** include; German Shepherd Dog and the Labrador retriever.

17.3.3 Luxating Patella

This is also known as **trick knee**, **subluxation of patella**, **floating patella**, or **floating kneecap** is a condition in which the patella, or kneecap, dislocates or moves out of its normal location. Patella luxation is a common condition in dogs, particularly small and miniature breeds. The condition usually becomes evident between the ages of 4 to 6 months. Dogs with this condition usually present themselves as a dog walking with a 'skip'. The dog walks into the salon and every step or two will skip by holding up the effected rear leg. Care is the same as a dog with a cruciate injury.

17.4 Cruciate Ligament Injury

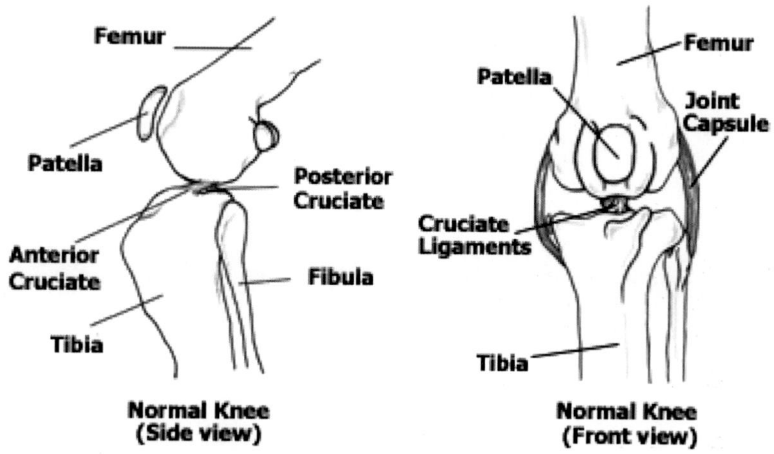

Cruciate Ligament injuries are one of the most common orthopaedic injuries that groomers see within the salon. The ligament connects the bone above the knee (the femur) with the bone below the knee (the tibia). Essentially stabilizes the knee (or stifle) joint. This can affect all dogs, no matter the size, breed, sex or age. All dogs can get a cruciate injury. That said, studies show that certain breeds are more prone to cruciate injuries. These include: Labrador Retriever, Poodle, Golden Retriever, Bichon Frise, German Shepherd Dog, Rottweiler and Great Dane. A Cruciate injury is extremely painful and affected dogs can experience pain simply whilst walking. A tear or rupture leads to joint swelling, pain and instability in the knee joint. If left untreated it will cause lameness in the affected leg and, ultimately, chronic irreversible degenerative joint changes. Treatment requires surgery. The good news is that there is a high success rate and dogs who receive surgical treatment can resume regular activities after rehabilitation. Other predispositions to cruciate ligament injury include, but are not limited to: -

- Dogs who are overweight
- Unfit dogs who engage in sudden, strenuous, irregular activity (e.g. weekend-only walkers!!)
- Male dogs neutered under five months old
- Dogs with conformational abnormalities (e.g. lacking muscle tone and proper muscular skeletal development in their rear legs)

Clinical signs of a cruciate injury may include:

- Lameness or weakness in one or both hind legs
- Limping or reluctance to use one or both hind legs
- Limping worsens with exercise and improves with rest
- Abnormal posture, especially over the back and hip areas
- Reluctance to get up, jump, run or go up and down stairs
- Stiffness and difficulty getting up in morning
- Sitting at an odd angle, with a hind leg slanted unusually off to one side
- Swelling around the knee joint
- Muscle atrophy in the affected limb

Tel: 01283 703043 Email: liza@heavenlyz.com

As previously discussed keeping floor, bath and table surfaces non-slip and having height adjustable work surfaces for ease of lifting and ensuring that the dog does not over extend its joints (e.g. via jumping) will all contribute to safe work environment.

17.5 Anatomical breed disorders

17.5.1 Rickets

Rickets is a condition that causes deformities, swelling of the joints and bending of the long bones in young growing animals. It is caused by: -

- Insufficient phosphorus in the diet (phosphorus is an important mineral which is a major component of bone along with calcium)
- Insufficient vitamin D in the diet (vitamin D is needed for normal absorption of minerals from the intestine, and for the release of minerals from bone)
- Insufficient sunlight (many animals can make their own vitamin D if they are exposed to natural sunlight)

In summary, the disease is caused by a nutritional deficiency, or an inability to absorb nutrients from the intestine due to insufficient vitamin D and minerals. The result is that the cartilage that forms a young animal's skeleton does not calcify properly, the bone does not become rigid and it does not develop normally in response to external forces. Eventually weight bearing, and movement causes bending deformities of the bones. Fortunately, pets fed on a complete, balanced ration get adequate amounts of minerals and vitamin D in their food and, so they do not develop rickets. Rickets is rare in the UK. When it is seen the animal may have been fed a homemade or a "fad" diet (recovery treatment can be successful by feeding adequate amounts of minerals and vitamin D) or where the animal has not had adequate exposure to natural light (e.g. in the instance of 'puppy farming'). If the condition is detected and treated before the bones have finished growing (before 6 months of age, dependant on breed) the deformity may be corrected during the remaining growth phase. However, if the bones have already stopped growing (after 9 months of age, dependant on breed), deformity is only likely to be corrected by surgery.

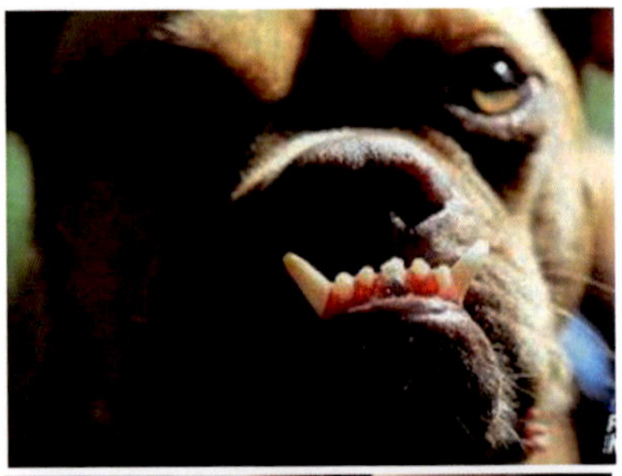

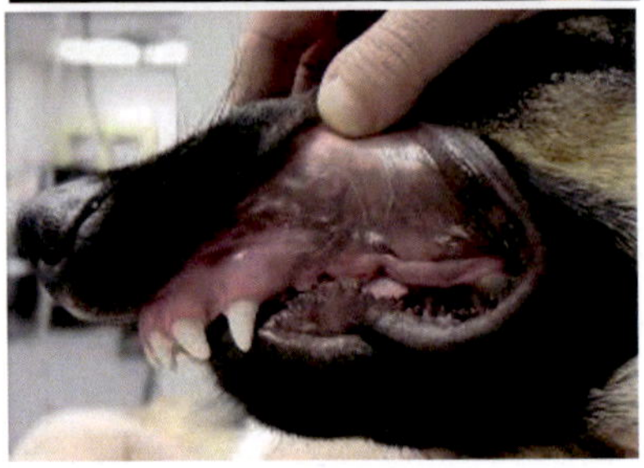

17.5.2 Jaw disorders

A normal jaw arrangement is where the upper jaw (maxilla) is aligned with the lower jaw (mandible). Where one jaw (either maxilla or mandible) is longer than it should be – this is called **Prognathism**. Where the lower jaw (mandible) is shorter than it should be causing an overshot bite, this is called **Brachygnathism**. Both undershot and overshot can be caused by Prognathism but only overshot is caused by Brachygnathism.

An undershot bite occurs when the lower jaw protrudes beyond the upper jaw. This is a bred abnormality, considered normal for Brachycephalic breeds, such as Bulldogs and Pugs.

An overshot bite occurs when the upper jaw protrudes beyond the lower jaw. **This is abnormal for any breed.**

17.6 Gastrointestinal Disorders

17.6.1 Gastric Dilation-Volvulus (Bloat or GDV)

GDV is a serious condition requiring urgent Veterinary attention. Commonly seen in large breed dogs with deep chests, it occurs when the dog's stomach becomes distended with air and, while the stomach is distended, it twists on itself. This interferes with the blood supply to the stomach and other organs, blocks passage of food and water and leads to the bloat worsening.

17.6.1.1 Signs of a Gastric Dilation

- Distended stomach
- Dog retches
- Restlessness
- Vomiting after drinking or eating
- Collapse

17.6.1.2 Increase Risk factors include;

- Overeating
- Rapid eating
- Single daily feeding

Tel: 01283 703043 Email: liza@heavenlyz.com

- High water consumption
- Stress
- Exercise before or after eating

For all deep chested breeds or those dogs who may be more easily susceptible to stress, it is advisable to restrict access to the amount of water consumed in a single instance. This is done to avoid over drinking (which could lead to a GDV). Where you are requested to feed the animal a diet that the owner has already provided, feed small amounts frequently. For large breeds, feeding from normal mouth height may reduce the possibility of taking in air whilst eating. There are commercially available bowls that have compartments which make the dog eat more slowly. Slowing the eating process is also thought to help reduce GDV. GDV primarily presents in deep chested breeds such as Great Dane, Standard Poodle, Irish Setter and St Bernard.

17.6.2 Perianal Fistula

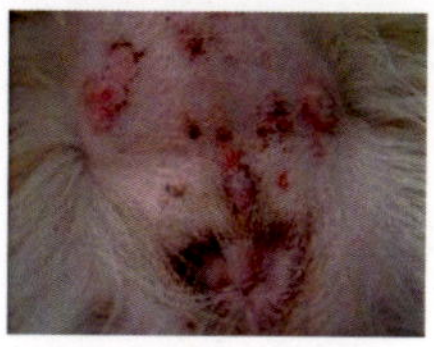

Perianal Fistula is a painful condition where single or multiple ulcerated tracts open in the tissue around the dog's anus. No clear cause has been established. Breeds affected by Perianal Fistula include the German Shepherd Dog.

17.7 Nervous System Disorders

17.7.1 Epilepsy

Epilepsy is a condition of seizures resulting from a nervous system imbalance. Seizures are typically seen between the ages of 1 to 3 years in dogs, although this will vary with different breeds. Breeds affected by Epilepsy include Golden Retriever, Labrador Retriever and Belgian Tervuren.

17.7.2 Deafness

Puppy dogs are born functionally deaf, most developing normal hearing function within weeks.

Puppies who do not develop fully functional hearing most commonly do so due to an inner ear deformation or lack of pigmented skin cells. Either can lead to early death of the nerve cells that need to develop for hearing to occur. In this case the nerve endings die in the first few weeks of the puppy's life and deafness ensues. This may occur in one or both ears. Dogs most likely to suffer from deafness share similar characteristics, especially merled or spotted coats/ blue eyes or pink skin (e.g. Border Collies, Bull Terriers, Dalmatians, English Setters, etc.).

Dogs can also become deaf during their lifetime. Dog deafness can occur gradually or suddenly, by injury, disease or simply old age.

The only reliable way to confirm impaired hearing in a dog is a specialist test, carried out by a vet or other suitably qualified expert.

17.7.3 Dilated Cardiomyopathy (DCM)

DCM is a disease affecting the heart muscle. It is the second most common heart disease in dogs (after mitral valve disease). In DCM the heart is unable to contract normally. DCM affects mainly middle-aged, large and giant breed dogs and some Spaniels. Small breeds of dog are occasionally affected. Male dogs are more likely to be affected than females. If you have a dog visiting the salon with a known heart condition, it is advisable to make the following adjustments to your daily routine: -

- Operate an appointment system to avoid either you or the dog from becoming stressed due to time restraint or overcrowding of the salon
- Avoid use of drying cabinet as this may have an impact on the dog's ability to regulate its own body temperature
- Offer the dog rest periods, as the dog's body language dictates, avoid making them stand for long periods of time
- For dogs requiring restraint, muzzling should be used with extreme caution preferred method would be for either the owner to stay and help handle or an employee.

Tel: 01283 703043 Email: liza@heavenlyz.com

18 Parasites

There are two different types of Parasites: -

- **Ectoparasites -** a parasite that lives outside of the dog's body (e.g. flea/ mite)
- **Endoparasites -** a parasite that lives its full life cycle or part of its life cycle inside the dog (e.g. worm)

The general prevention against worms and parasites can be summarised as follows.

- Dogs should be wormed every four months and more regularly if parasite infestation occurs
- Minimise exposure to fleas and lice
- Dispose of faeces immediately
- Disinfect areas contaminated by faeces
- Wash hands after handling an animal (and especially before handling another animal)
- Wash animal bowls away from human utensils
- Do not let animals lick your face
- Keep animal's anal area clean
- Examine faeces passed for signs of worms or abnormalities such as blood, mucous
- Regular grooming to examine for fleas/lice

However, prevention is not a guarantee and the following content describes parasites in more detail.

18.1 Ectoparasites

18.1.1 FLEA (Ctenocephalides)

Fleas are blackish brown and shiny in appearance. They live on animals where they inflict bites with their mouth parts to feed off the blood of the animal.

Fleas are often found in clusters behind ears and other sparse haired areas, where feeding is made easier with lack of hair follicles. They run about the body rapidly, rather than jumping.

18.1.1.1 Flea Detection

Black dirt can be seen on fur or in dogs bedding, usually mistaken for eggs. However, this is in fact flea faeces (mainly digested blood).

Confirm the presence of fleas by collecting some of this dirt onto piece of white paper. Add a drop of water to the dirt. If it turns a bloody brown, then consider this to be a strong indication of the presence of fleas.

18.1.1.2 Indications of Fleas

- Flea dirt/ fleas visible on animal's coat
- Dog scratching and excess licking
- Many animals are allergic to flea saliva and their skin may be enflamed/ reddened from flea bites
- Hair loss from excessive over grooming/ self-mutilation
- Dogs quickly looking at base of tail
- Obvious signs of distress and anxiety

18.1.1.3 Treatment of Flea on the infected dog whilst in the salon

- If possible, prevent the cross contamination of other dogs in the salon by grooming the infected dog in a separate area. If this is not possible, you should consider whether it is fair to risk contamination of other animals.
- Immediately after use, thoroughly clean all equipment
- Collect all hair and place in a plastic bag seal to prevent fleas jumping out

Tel: 01283 703043 Email: liza@heavenlyz.com

- Phone owner to inform and double check that they have not applied treatment recently to avoid overdosing the animal (usually the owner is aware of the problem and has in fact, before visiting the salon, treated with a topical product).
- Once animal groomed out, bath, either used an insecticidal shampoo if no other topical application has been used or alternatively after the shampoo stage. Apply generous amount of conditioner, comb through the coat whilst dog is in bath to remove all fleas and flea dirt.
- Rinse and dry as usual
- Ensure the environment is warm to avoid the dog being uncomfortable whilst wet and being combed through.
- Advise owners to: -
    - consult a veterinary surgeon
    - treat the house for infestation (fleas can live up to two years)
    - worm the dog (the flea is an intermediate host of the tapeworm)
- Change your clothing after handling dog and boil wash to kill any eggs. Fleas are Zoonotic and will feed off Humans.

18.1.2 TICK (Ixodes)

Ticks climb onto a passing animal to feed on the animal's blood; they bury their mouth part into the epidermis/ skin, and feed until engorged where they physically drop off the host. Diseases are transmitted from the tick's saliva includes Lyme disease (a Bacteria that causes skin discolouration on the site of the bite), joint disease and cardiac disease. Symptoms of tick infestation include: -

- Sudden onset lameness and pain to one or more joints
- High temperature

To remove a tick, use a specially manufactured tick remover. **Caution:** when attached to an animal, the Tick's mouth parts are buried into the animal's skin. When removing the tick ensure that it is not decapitated as this will leave the mouth buried, leading to infection and pain.

Gently place the remover between the animal's skin and ticks body. Apply gentle but consistent uplifting force, enough to allow the tick to stop biting and let go of its grip, but not too much to decapitate it, some commercial available tick removers also require a twist motion. Read instructions carefully or ask your veterinary professional to demonstrate until you feel proficient.

18.1.3 Lice

Lice are slow moving and attach themselves to the animal's skin where they feed on blood (Sucking Louse), hair and dead skin (Biting Louse). There are two types of lice: -

- Biting Louse
- Sucking Louse

Symptoms of live infestation include: -

- Skin irritation and inflammation
- Alopecia
- Scabs on skin
- Visibly be seen on dog's coat with naked eye.

The treatment for a dog with a confirmed lice infestation is as follows: -

- Separate all equipment and isolate dog
- Sterilise all equipment once dog left salon
- Advice seeks veterinary treatment

Tel: 01283 703043 Email: liza@heavenlyz.com

18.1.4 Sarcoptes Mites

Symptoms of Sarcoptes Mites include inflammation and self-inflicted injury to affected areas (usually ears, muzzle, face, elbows). Note that Sarcoptes mites are zoonotic and will infect humans.

The treatment for a dog with a confirmed Sarcoptes Mite infestation is as follows: -

- If you suspect Sarcoptes, ensure adequate PPE is worn and basic hygiene is carried out
- Isolate infected dog away from other animals
- Remove infected dog from salon **as soon as possible**
- Advise owner to seek veterinary attention
- Thoroughly disinfect all areas of salon with which the dog has had contact.

18.1.5 Cheyletiella Mites

This mite is often known as 'walking dandruff' as it can be seen with the naked eye. It causes skin irritation which is excessive scurf or dandruff.

18.1.6 Demodex Mite

A long cigar shaped Mite, microscopic, usually seen on animals that are stressed or debilitated, or on young animals (these mites are often transferred from mother to young). Symptoms of the Demodex mite include: -

- Hair loss on face particularly around eyes
- Skin thickens
- Inflammation of and discharge from skin.

The treatment for the Demodex Mite is the same as that for the Sarcoptes Mite.

18.1.7 Harvest Mite (Trombicula autumnalis)

Usually a problem in late summer/ autumn. Bright orange and round, usually localised to face, muzzle, ears, feet and legs. This mite bites the dog's skin and injects an enzyme, which then breaks down the skin around the bite area, causing inflammation and infection. Treat as for Sarcoptes mite and advise the owner to consult a veterinary surgeon.

18.1.8 Ear Mite (Otodectes Cynotis)

Symptoms;

- Head shaking and ear scratching
- On examination of ear canal, excessive brownish waxy secretion can be seen
- Inflammation and pain

Treatment

- Advice owner seeks advice of a veterinary surgeon;
- Do not clean out ear as you will remove evidence for the vet to make a diagnosis on!

18.2 Endoparasites

Signs of Internal parasites;

- Poor coat condition/ unhealthy dull coat
- The dog is constantly hungry, and though eating properly may still be losing weight
- Enlarged abdomen (particularly seen in the young)
- Vomiting
- Diarrhoea
- Constipation
- Irritation, especially anal irritation (presented as the dog shuffling along on its bottom)
- Burping
- Coughing

The following sections describe the commonest type of Endoparasites that may be encountered in the grooming salon.

18.2.1 Roundworm (Nematode or Ascarids)

Unsegmented bodies, yellow/ white in colour with both ends are pointed (it resembles spaghetti). The most common round worm is the Toxocara Cani round worm. This is transmissible to humans, is linked to blindness and human diseases called Toxocariasis.

Common round worms in dogs are Toxocaris Leonina and Toxocaris Canis

Toxocariasis is a rare infection caused by roundworm parasites. It is spread from animals to humans via their infected faeces.

Roundworm parasites are most commonly found in cats, dogs and foxes and usually affect young children. The roundworm parasites responsible for Toxocariasis are called Toxocara. Most cases make a full recovery and don't experience any long-term complications. However, there is a risk of permanent vision loss if one of the eyes is affected.

The following table describes types of nematode. Prevention for all the following is ensuring that the environment is always clean (regularly cleaned), that waste (urine & faeces) are removed as early as possible, water bowls, food bowls and outside toys are cleaned daily and that an effective worm control programme is maintained.

Name	UK presence	Name of infection(s) in dogs	Notes re. infection in dogs	Transmission	Clinical signs	Treatment	Zoonotic?
Heart worm	Predominantly found in northern American dogs imported to the UK	Dirofilariasis	Young worms circulate in blood vessels and can block the flow of blood causing damage to internal organs (notably heart, lungs and liver). Mature worms can be found in the heart between 6-14 inches/ 15-35 cm in size	Predominantly transmitted by mosquito	Dry chronic cough Shortness of cough Weakness Listlessness Low/ lost stamina	Blood test/ X-ray/ ECG to diagnose. Injectable drugs (antibiotic, heart specific and other prophylactics)	No
Whip worm	Uncommon	Trichuris Vulpis	Live in the large intestine. Thin front end shaped like a whip and thick rear end shaped like a whip handle	Contaminated eating or drinking Can survive outside for several years and is resistant to extreme temperatures (e.g. freezing)	Diarrhoea containing blood Weight loss Inflamed large bowel	Oral medication Dehydration treatment if diarrhoea is significant/ prolonged	Yes

Tel: 01283 703043 Email: liza@heavenlyz.com

Name	UK presence	Name of infection(s) in dogs	Notes re. infection in dogs	Transmission	Clinical signs	Treatment	Zoonotic?
Hook worm	Common	Uncinariasis Stenocephala and Ancylostoma Caninum	Short, blood sucking parasite, with teeth. Circulates around body until it reaches the lungs, from where it is coughed up and re-ingested back into the intestines	Contaminated eating or drinking Prevalent in wet or moist areas	Blood in faeces Dry, itchy, skin/ Dermatitis Diarrhoea Vomit-like aroma	Oral medication Hygienic sanitation	Yes
Thread worm	Common	Strongyloides Stercoralis	Extremely thin parasite with thread like appearance Resides & reproduces in intestine. Hatched eggs/ larvae pass out in faeces	Contact, especially dogs living in dirty, overcrowded conditions. Puppies suckling milk from an infected mother are also at risk	Some dogs do not present symptoms. Other dogs will have diarrhoea, persistent coughing	Oral medication	Yes
Lung worm	Common	Angiostrongylus Vasorum	Lives in heart and the major blood vessels supplying the lungs	Carried in slugs, snails, puddles and grass This is not passed from dog to dog	Coughing (n.b. fatal if not treated)	Blood tests, x-rays, bronchoscopy	No

Email: liza@heavenlyz.com

18.2.2 Tapeworm (Cestode)

A tapeworm has a segmented body. These segments break off and are passed out with faeces, resembling grains of rice. Fleas are intermediate hosts for the worm eggs in the life cycle of the tape worm. Tapeworms common to dogs are **Dipylidium Caninum**.

18.2.3 Toxoplasma Gondii

Toxoplasma Gondii is a microscopic, single-cell, organism that can be found in meat, cat faeces, soil which has been previously defecated upon and unpasteurised goat's milk.

This parasite can infect most birds and warm-blooded animals, including humans. Cats are the only animals that can have infected faeces. Toxoplasmosis is only a public health risk to an unborn baby if caught for the first time during pregnancy or within a few weeks prior to conception. An unborn baby who contracts the disease is said to have congenital toxoplasmosis. The degree of risk to the foetus, and the damage caused, depends on when in pregnancy the mother acquired the infection.

18.2.4 Toxoplasmosis Coccidiosis

Usually occurs when dogs are kept in confined, overcrowded, conditions and especially where dogs drink Coccidia contaminated water.

Coccidia is a (protozoan) parasite and one of a range of parasites that can lead to Coccidiosis, other digestive ailments and health problems. Although it can affect any dog at any age, it is common in the young and in dogs who are stressed or have a suppressed immune system.

Coccidiosis can be passed from a dam to her puppies, and the infection can also pass from dog to dog by contact with faecal matter. This can include direct contact with faeces, or indirect contact, such as with objects or animals that have minute traces of faeces or faecal bacteria present on the surface of the object or the body.

The most obvious symptom of Coccidiosis in dogs is diarrhoea. The diarrhoea of a dog suffering with a Coccidia infection is likely to be very runny, mucous-like, and often uncontrollable. During the later stages of infection, there may be blood in the diarrhoea, the dog will possibly be suffering from dehydration and being in a generally unwell and weakened state. Diagnosis and treatment will require a sample of stools to be examined by a veterinary surgeon for the presence of the parasite.

18.2.5 Leishmaniasis

Leishmaniasis is caused by a protozoan transmitted from the sand fly. It is endemic to the Mediterranean, Middle East and Sub Tropical regions. The parasite invades white cells. Leishmaniasis is Zoonotic and causes weight loss, skin disease, joint pain, fever and kidney damage.

Tel: 01283 703043 Email: liza@heavenlyz.com

19 Fungal Infection (Ring Worm)

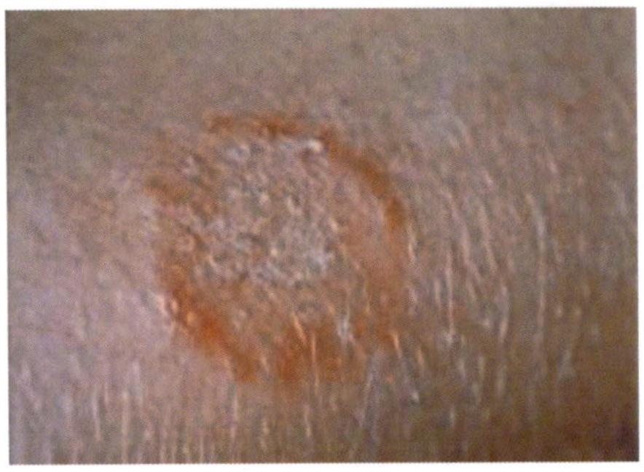

Despite its title, ring worm is not caused by a worm – it is caused by a fungal infection. The fungus lives on the surface of the skin and in the hair follicles, feeding on dead skin tissue and hair. The main fungus in dogs is **called Microsporum Canis**.

Ring worm appears as a hairless lesion. The characteristic "ring" seen on humans doesn't always appear as a ring on dogs. This lesion will grow and often become irregular in shape. The fungi cause the hair shafts to break off and this results in patches of hair loss. Ringworm are commonly found on the face, ears, tail and paws. The lesions are scaly and may, or may not, be itchy. Often the skin is reddened and inflamed.

Transmission can happen by direct contact with another infected animal or person. It can be passed between dogs and cats either way as well as between pets and humans, also either way.

The fungal spores can live in the environment for a long time and can be found in carpets, bedding, grooming equipment, etc., all of which can infect your dog if it encounters them. The ringworm incubation period is 10-12 days. This means that following exposure to the fungus, about 10-12 days will pass before any lesions occur. Humans can catch ringworm by touching a dog infected with ringworm.

Tel: 01283 703043 Email: liza@heavenlyz.com

20 Disease

20.1 Dog to dog contact

Some salons operate a waiting-in-pens policy, other salons operate a free-roaming policy, this is a choice made by salon management, both policies are defensible and either choice has both advantages and disadvantages. However, to prevent the spread of infection and disease, direct contact between dogs from different households should be avoided.

Remember to wash your hands between handling different dogs to help prevent the spread of infection. It may be useful to have an alcoholic gel sanitizer placed on the wall for quick hand cleansing. Operating a grooming where fully vaccinated only policy would reduce risk of disease spreading in the salon. However, this alone does not replace the importance of all dogs being health checked prior to a groom being carried out.

Where unvaccinated dogs are to be accepted for grooming, Heavenlyz recommends that they attend the salon at the end of the day and after a point when all vaccinated dogs have left (e.g. when the salon has closed). A thorough clean, ready for the next day, is advisable after an unvaccinated dog leaves the salon.

20.2 Disease Prevention

Dogs are vaccinated against known, and common, infectious diseases. Puppies receive a primary course of vaccines at approximately 8/ 9 and 10/ 12 weeks. Typically, animals are not fully immunised until 5 days after the last vaccine (though a qualified veterinarian may modify the immunisation term based on the specific vaccine being applied).

Typically, following a vaccine, an annual top up ("booster") vaccine is recommended. This is because for some of the diseases mentioned above, immunity is short-lived. This is especially true in the case of Leptospirosis. For other diseases, such as distemper and adenovirus, the immunity lasts longer, so it is recommend vaccinating against these diseases every 2 years. Please seek advice from your own veterinary surgeon. The following canine diseases have readily available vaccines: -

- Distemper
- Hepatitis
- Leptospirosis
- Parvovirus
- Para-influenza (can lead to kennel cough)
- Rabies
- Bordetella Bronchiseptica (can lead to kennel cough)

Tel: 01283 703043 Email: liza@heavenlyz.com

20.3 Common Diseases

The following table describes in general terms the key attributes of diseases commonly found by the dog groomer.

Name of animal disease	Name of same disease if found in humans	Route of Transmission	Incubation period	Clinical signs	Zoonotic
Canine Distemper	NA	Direct contact nose to mouth and aerosol Airborne exposure	3-10 days	High body temperature for 2-3 days Lack of appetite Nasal and eye discharge Coughing Diarrhoea and vomiting Hardening of the footpads Inco-ordination Paralysis Fits	no
Canine Hepatitis	NA	Direct nose to nose contact	5-9 days	Puppies develop high temperature and death occurs within hours Older dogs develop blood stained vomit and diarrhoea, acute abdominal pain and in some dogs 'blue eye'/ cloudy cornea occurs	no
Canine Infectious Tracheobronchitis (Kennel Cough)	NA	Direct nose to nose contact Airborne exposure	3-7 days	Coughing Sneezing Depressed but still eating Retching after coughing	no

Email: liza@heavenlyz.com

Name of animal disease	Name of same disease if found in humans	Route of Transmission	Incubation period	Clinical signs	Zoonotic
Canine Leptospirosis	Weils Disease	Direct contact Ingestion of infected water	7-21 days	High temp Shivering muscle pains Vomiting and diarrhoea Dehydration Shock Jaundice (mucous membranes mouth and eye yellow)	yes
Canine Parvovirus	NA	Faecal and oral contact	5-10 days	Dull and depressed Anorexia High temp Vomiting Blood stained diarrhoea/vomit Dehydration	no
Cheyletiella mites	Cheyletiella Mites	Direct contact	NA	Parasite bite	Yes
Rabies	Rabies	Direct contact	10 days – 4 months	Three stages of disease: - Preclinical raised temperature, slow eye reflexes and irritation. Excitable; irritable, aggressive and disorientated Dumb stage; animals throat and muscles progressively paralyse leading to excess salivation, difficulty breathing and death	yes
Ringworm	Ringworm	Direct Contact	10-12 days	Raised circular inflamed skin lesions	Yes

Tel: 01283 703043 Email: liza@heavenlyz.com

Name of animal disease	Name of same disease if found in humans	Route of Transmission	Incubation period	Clinical signs	Zoonotic
Salmonella	Salmonella	Direct contact/ingestion		Gastroenteritis	Yes
Sarcoptic Mange	Scabies	Direct Contact	NA	Skin rash and bites	Yes
Toxocariasis	Round worm parasite	Direct Contact	NA	Head ache, stomach pain, visual disturbance	Yes
Von Willibrand disease	Von Willibrand disease	NA	NA	Excessive bleeding in the mouth Excessive bleeding after surgery Greater than expected bleeding times before healing	No

Email: liza@heavenlyz.com

21 Care of a Sick Dog

All sick dogs must EITHER: -

- be sent home with owners OR
- if fit enough and it is the most appropriate option, be transported to a veterinary surgeon OR
- if not fit enough, receive veterinary surgeon attendance onsite at the salon

Be aware that the owner may not be contactable before veterinary intervention – this reinforces the importance of holding owners consent to treat their pet at your discretion.

Whilst the animal is in the salon, observe the following: -

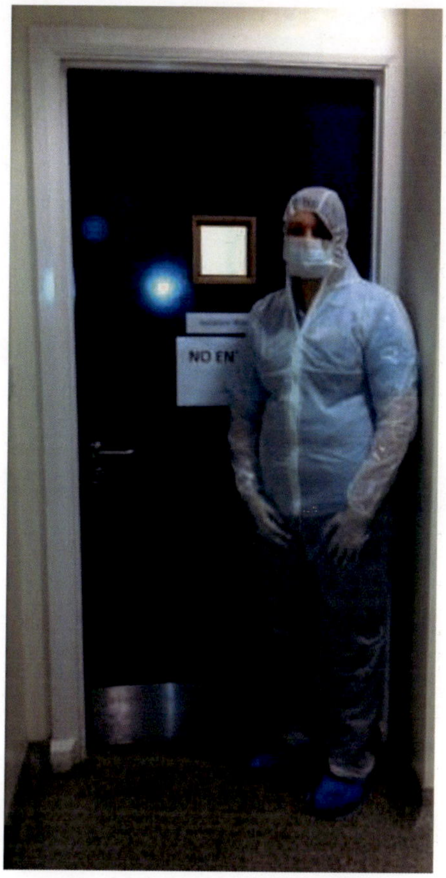

- make the dog as comfortable as possible
- employ 'Barrier Nursing'. Barrier Nursing means placing a barrier between the ill dog and its wider environment, other dogs and humans to prevent further spread of possible infectious illness. This barrier may be physical, biological, other or a mix of different barrier types.
- place the dog in a quiet, comfortable, bedded, holding unit and constantly observe.
- practice good hygiene to prevent any possible spread of infection by washing hands properly and disinfecting any equipment that has had contact with the ill dog.
- thoroughly disinfect all areas in contact with ill dog once dog has left premises.
- create a temporary and separate isolation facility in your salon. Some disease and infections are airborne and spread by respiratory droplet transmission. This is unavoidable in a closed salon. However, we can try and separate any suspected diseased dogs from well dogs/ prevent direct contact spread by creating a temporary isolation area whilst you wait for the owner to collect the potentially infectious dog. Creating a temporary isolation can be achieved by the following: -
    - allocate a member of staff to care for the potentially infectious dog. Until all their clothing and personal hygiene has been cleaned, this staff member will not handle other dogs.
    - Cordon off/ tape off an area that is to be the isolated area. This could be a simple as a corner of the room, where tape has been placed on the floor or a temporary barricade put in place.
    - Make a foot disinfecting bath. This can be created by placing a tray, perhaps a cat litter tray, onto a non-slip surface (e.g. a rubber matt). Place newspaper at the bottom of the tray and fill up with correctly diluted disinfectant. The designated person should use this to dip their foot wear in as they enter or leave the area to help spread of infection
    - The designated person should wear PPE, including gloves, apron, etc. This should be taken off, in a controlled process, at the exit of the isolation site to avoid the cross contamination of other dogs within the same area
    - Hand sterilisation facilities. Provide this such via a non-alcoholic gel or [bucket of] skin friendly detergent, placing it near the exit of the isolation site.
    - Warn all staff members that the temporarily cordoned off area is a no-go area
    - Thoroughly sterilise and disinfect the affected area once the dog leaves the building
    - Remember to keep all cleaning mops and buckets, water and food bowls, lead etc. separate from all other dogs in the salon and disinfect thoroughly once dog goes home
- Isolate the dog in the isolation area and away from other dogs to prevent spread of infection

Tel: 01283 703043 Email: liza@heavenlyz.com

22 First-Aid and Emergencies

We will first concentrate on First Aid and Emergencies as they apply to animals in your care. The 1966 veterinary surgeons act prevents anyone from practising veterinary surgery unless registered as a veterinary surgeon. However, if an emergency arises it is permissible to give first-aid treatment to the animal. This should only be carried out until the veterinary surgeon is able to attend. The aims of first-aid are: -

- to preserve life
- to prevent the situation deteriorating
- to prevent suffering

The four rules of first-aid are: -

1. Do not panic
2. Maintain the Airway
3. Control any Haemorrhaging (bleeding)
4. Contact a vet ASAP

Before opening a salon makes sure you have: -

- Appropriate Insurance (e.g. consider the scenario where an otherwise healthy dog is injured in your salon)
- A well-stocked, well-maintained animal first aid kit
- Signed owner authority to obtain vet treatment for their pet in case of emergency.
- Attended a reputable pet first aid course
- Sourced a pet first-aid kit, to include: -
    - Sterile gauze pads (3" x 3" and 2" X 2")
    - Tweezers
    - Scissors
    - Antiseptic wipes
    - Latex gloves
    - Selection of bandaging materials to include conforming bandage and cotton wool bandage
    - Forceps
    - Saline solution
    - Micropore tape
    - Foil blanket
    - Tick remover
    - CPCR mask
    - Rectal thermometer
- Operating an appointment system is recommended –the advantages of this facility include reduction of (i) dogs awaiting collection after grooming and (ii) the time that a dog is exposed to the potentially stressful situation that the salon may present.

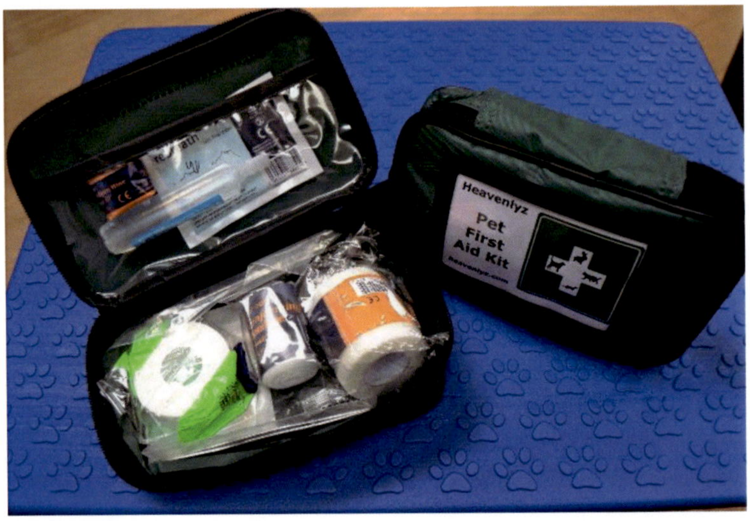

In summary, if the dog is sick or injured in the salon: -

- Take appropriate action to avoid a life-threatening situation
- Inform the owner as early as possible
- If emergency; take dog to the Vets
- If not emergency; ask owner if they wish to take their dog to the vets
- Contact insurance company if you are liable (e.g. injury caused at salon)
- Follow up with owner to see if dog fully recovered

22.1 Approaching an Injured Dog

- Use slow deliberate actions and reassure the dog
- Approach from the side (rather than head on, which may be interpreted as a threat)

Tel: 01283 703043 Email: liza@heavenlyz.com

- If the dog is in a dangerous area, it may be necessary to place a slip lead round the pet and pull it to a safe area
- If the dog is in pain, has no respiratory problems and the injury is not to the mouth, then for your safety only, a muzzle may be used.

22.2 Moving an Injured Dog

If the dog is small and can be carried, transfer it to the veterinary practice in a pet carrier. If the pet is large and able to walk, then secure it appropriately (e.g. via collar and lead) and walk at dog's own pace. If you suspect spinal/ neck injury, then attempt to immobilise the dog, place on a board or make an impromptu stretcher (e.g. use of blanket or towel) – try to keep the dog immobile.

22.3 Common Salon Emergencies

22.3.1 Bleeding

Dogs can bleed from: -

- Arteries (Bright red and pumping)
- Veins (Darker red not pumping)
- Capillaries (oozing)

For any type of bleeding wound, note the following caution: -

- never remove any bandage if they become blood soaked, as this may dislodge any clots. Instead, simply bandage directly onto the original bandage.
- do not remove any penetrating object. Instead, bandage around the object being careful no too push it further into the wound.

22.3.1.1 Arterial bleeding

Arterial bleeding is bright red and spurts – this is the most serious type of bleeding. Take the following action: -

- Apply pressure over the wound and bandage.
- Do not remove bandage if blood seeps through, keep adding more pressure with clean bandaging onto a bandage already applied.
- This type of bleeding requires vet treatment immediately.

22.3.1.2 Venous bleeding

Venous bleeding is darker red and will flow steadily – this type of bleeding is also serious. Take the following action: -

- Apply pressure and bandage
- Seek vet treatment

22.3.1.3 Capillary bleeding

Capillary bleeding is light and oozes with little force. Take the following action: -

- Apply pressure and bandage.
- Seek vet treatment

22.3.2 Wounds

There are several different types of wounds: -

- **Incised wounds** – These are clean with defined edges caused by sharps such as glasses, knives or scissors.
- **Lacerated wounds** – Irregular with jagged edges caused by a tearing action (e.g. barbed wire, clippers), they can time to heal.
- **Puncture wounds** – Small hole or puncture caused by nails, thorns or teeth, these can become infected especially if from bite wounds.

Tel: 01283 703043 Email: liza@heavenlyz.com

- **Abrasions** – A graze which does not penetrate the entire skin thickness, like gravel rash.
- **Contused** – A bruise caused by ruptured blood vessels in the skin seeping blood to surrounding tissue.

In all cases, bandaging may be required: -

- In an emergency to control haemorrhage
- To prevent infection
- Prevent pet chewing or licking at wound

22.3.2.1 General Wounds

Minor grazes and cuts are commonly seen. If minor, clean and apply a coagulant. Advise owner to check daily in case of infection.

22.3.2.2 Clipper and scissor cuts

Calm the dog down. Once you notice that the dog is injured, reassure them, control them and, if over-excited, calm them. Soothe the dog by petting them gently and speaking to them in a low, calm voice. Make sure to stay calm yourself, even if you're worried (the dog can read your body language and understands voice intonations, they will pick up on your behaviour and follow your lead).

One reason for calming the dog as much as possible is that blood flows as fast as the heart pumps. By calming the dog, you are also slowing the heart and the blood flow (and potentially reducing loss of blood).

If you feel ill prepared or inexperienced seek advice of colleagues, management or vets.

Unless the dog has mouth injuries or breathing difficulties, **consider muzzling the dog if necessary.** You need to keep your own safety in mind when handling an injured animal. Even if the dog is normally sweet and loving, he/ she may lash out to protect from further pain. If you're at all worried for your safety, if the dog starts growling or snapping or if the dog has a previous history of biting when agitated, then muzzle the dog.

Address any bleeding you see. It is vital to stop profuse bleeding as soon as possible. If blood seems to be ***pulsing*** out of the wound, the dog may have an arterial injury that could be very dangerous; pulsing blood should be taken very seriously.

- Apply direct pressure to the wound using a clean, absorbent material like a towel, washcloth, shirt, gauze (even a feminine hygiene pad) – we'll term this the "dressing"
- Keep pressure on the wound for 3-5 minutes before checking to see if the bleeding has stopped. If you keep taking the pressure off, you may disturb the blood clot that is forming and delay the process
- If the bleed comes through the dressing, do not remove the dressing. Add another dressing on top and call a vet for **immediate** intervention. Keep pressure/ dressing(s) on the wound until bleeding stops or you are instructed otherwise by the vet.

In the case of a capillary or superficial venous bleed the bleeding should stop where pressure and dressing(s) are applied. Use of skin glues or other generally available options generally available are not recommended. Instead, monitor the wound and seek veterinary advice.

Arterial bleeds or deep venous bleeds may not stop bleeding with digital pressure/ dressing(s). The application of a tourniquet may be your only option, and this should be a last resort only unless you're under expert instruction. Applying a tourniquet incorrectly can lead to complications that might result in tissue death. Your pet might need amputation if you cut off circulation. If you don't have training in applying a tourniquet to a dog, call your vet for expert instruction.

- Place a clean towel or pad around the limb (but not around the neck, chest, or abdomen).
- Use a belt or leash to hold it in place. It should be placed above the wound, toward the body.
- Leave it on for no more than 5 to 10 minutes before releasing the pressure to avoid permanent injury to the limb.
- Use enough pressure to slow down or stop the bleeding but avoid crushing the muscle and soft tissue.
- Applying the tourniquet should not be painful to your pet and only done under veterinary instruction

Tel: 01283 703043 Email: liza@heavenlyz.com

22.3.2.3 Ears

Ear injuries may bleed significantly. If minor apply pressure for at least 5 minutes or as long as dog will tolerate. Throughout this time keep the pressure on, do not keeping stopping to inspect. Once the bleeding is manageable, clean and apply a coagulant/ wound sealer.

Advise owner to check daily in case of infection.

If wound is deep or large, apply bandage and seek vet treatment.

When bandaging a single ear, if a dog has: -

- **non-pricked** ears - pad with cotton wool on top of the dog's head and gently flip the ear back onto pad on top of the dog's head
- **pricked** ears – gently bandage using padding to form natural ear position

Apply a bandage onto the head. Take care not to apply too tightly under the chin, it is important that the dog can open its mouth normally and respiration is not impaired.

Where ears are covered by bandages, mark the position of the ear on the bandage to help prevent accidental damage to the ear when the bandage is later removed.

22.3.2.4 Tongues

Tongue injuries can happen if a pet licks the clipper blade or bites its tongue. To treat, if the dog will allow, hold a sterile gauze pad against the wound until bleeding stops. If bleeding doesn't stop within ten minutes, reapply the pressure and seek veterinary surgeon's advice. Do not use sealing products, especially liquid glue.

22.3.2.5 Nails

Pour some styptic powder or corn-starch/ powder (with or without baking soda) into the palm. Gently dip the dog's bleeding nail into the powder, repeating this if the bleeding doesn't come to an immediate stop. Don't wipe away the blood before dipping because it will aid coagulation. Once bleeding does cease, continue to compress the wound with a paper towel or cloth, being cautious not to squeeze the paw. Try to keep the dog off his feet for at least 30 minutes.

Once you are sure that the dog nail bleeding has been stopped, wash the affected nail with lukewarm water and bandage to prevent licking and infection. If bleeding cannot be controlled after 20 – 30 minutes, proper clotting is not taking place and a veterinarian should be consulted immediately. Also consult a vet if the dog's toe later becomes red, swollen or does not appear to be improving after a few days.

Usually, if severe, the clot will form after application of 'quick stop'. However, as soon as the dog walks, the clot may dislodge, and the nail may bleed again. Consider bandaging the foot for at least an hour to help the clot to form. Remove the bandage before returning the dog to the owner. If still worried visit vet or ask owner to visit vet at your expense.

22.3.2.6 Sprains and Strains

A sprain is an injury when a joint has been forced violently too far in one direction. A strain is the stretching or tearing of a muscle or tendon. Both can happen within the grooming environment. Care should be taken not to put pressure on the dog's limbs when restraining. Safety procedures should be followed to avoid accidental jumping from tables and bathing area. If you suspect an injury of a limb treat as follows: -

- Restrict the dog's movement
- Apply a suitable support dressing
- Transport to the veterinary surgeons

22.3.3 Aural Haematomas

Haematoma is commonly seen in pets with ear problems. They can also occur through rigorous head shaking in the salon when we have removed heavy matts/ coat from an ear or accidentally allowed water or hair to enter the ear canal.

Dogs with ear problems, that then shake their heads, can cause a haematoma. This is due to the blood vessels rupturing within the ear flap (the "Pinna") and fluid filling the ear pocket, creating a balloon.

Tel: 01283 703043 Email: liza@heavenlyz.com

To avoid further damage, this requires veterinary attention immediately.

To Prevent Haematomas, head shaking during and after the grooming process must be discouraged. Heavenlyz recommend Happy Hoodies for this purpose (they also seem to relax dogs).

To treat Haematomas: -

- Either: -
  - Properly bandage the affected ear to prevent further damage Or
  - Apply a cold compress if bandaging is impractical
- Transport to Veterinary surgeon

22.3.4 Epistaxis

"Nosebleed" ...Epistaxis refers to bleeding from the nose that may be caused by trauma, a foreign body, persistent sneezing, infection or a tumour (cancer). The Clinical signs of Epistaxis are: -

- Haemorrhage from the nostrils
- Sneezing blood-tinged fluid
- Mouth breathing
- Difficulty breathing
- Swelling

To treat Epistaxis: -

- Place ice pack over muzzle/ nasal passages
- With soft cotton plug the nostril (but only if one nostril only affected – **do not plug both at the same time!** Dogs are not natural mouth breathers and may panic if both nostrils are blocked at the same time. This is especially important to observe for Brachycephalic breeds).
- Keep the animal calm and quiet
- If bleeding is recurrent, prolonged or profuse (severe), seek veterinary care as soon as possible
- **Do not squeeze nostrils together**

22.3.5 Detergent in eyes

For example, shampoo getting into the animal's eye. To treat this: -

- Rinse immediately with clean water.
- Check the area especially the eyes for any signs of redness.
- Should the animal start pawing at its eyes, to prevent self-trauma, apply an Elizabethan collar
- Transport to the veterinary surgeon.

22.3.6 Prolapse Eyeball ("**Proptosis**")

This can be caused by trauma (e.g. dog fight), inappropriate handling (e.g. over-scruffing a dog with protuberant eyes) or inappropriate use of high velocity dryer or disease.

Proptosis requires immediate veterinary attention.

Prior to veterinary support, Proptosis can be treated by: -

- Keeping the eye wet by applying sterile water. Apply with care and avoid touching the eyeball. The eyeball must not be allowed to dry out.
- Treat for Shock
- Place a buster collar on the dog to prevent self-interference
- Transport to the Veterinary Practice Immediately

Tel: 01283 703043 Email: liza@heavenlyz.com

22.3.7 Insect Stings

A Bee's sting is barbed and will be left behind by the bee. A Wasp's sting is straight and will invariably be removed by the Wasp on exit. Pets are often stung in the mouth whilst trying to catch insects and, if swelling continues in the throat and mouth area, this can cause respiratory obstruction. If stung in the mouth, seek veterinary advice whilst carrying out first aid measures. In all sting cases, follow this additional advice: -

- Inspect area to see if sting present and its poisonous sac remains.
- Remove the sting by scraping the string away from the skin (do not grasp the sting with tweezers, as this could empty the sac of poison into the skin, causing further damage).
- For Bee stings wash the affected area with an alkaline solution, one dessertspoon bicarbonate of soda to half litre of water.
- For Wasp sting wash affected area with dilute solution of vinegar (four-parts water to one-part vinegar)
- Once the area is washed, apply ice packs to alleviate pain and swelling
- If swelling does not respond to above measures transport to veterinary surgeon

22.3.8 Feet - Lick Granuloma

Caused by dog constantly licking an area until it becomes raw and inflamed, most common areas are the lower fore leg joints and toes. Over licking can be related to a habit-forming behaviour commonly seen in bored or stressed dogs. Large active breeds seem to be most affected for example Great Danes, Labrador Retrievers and English Springer Spaniels. To treat a lick granuloma: -

- Avoid drawing attention to the area and go around the area when grooming.
- If infected, cover the area with a suitable dressing
- Consider prevention on self-trauma whilst in your care by applying an Elizabethan collar
- Report to the owner and advise they seek veterinary attention

22.3.9 Burns and Scalds

A Burn is caused by extreme dry heat, extreme cold, corrosive material or electricity. A **scald** is caused by moist heat (e.g. steam). To treat either: -

- Cool area with water (do not use cream, ointments or powders)
- If applicable, remove any chemical residues from coat
- Prevent self-grooming/ chemical ingestion
- Keep animal warm and treat for shock
- Dress wound(s)
- Transport to veterinary surgeon

22.3.10 Brush Burns/ Clipper Burns

22.3.10.1 Cause

Both brush burns/ clipper burns are caused by intense dry heat.

A brush burn occurs when a groomer uses a brush to excessively and repetitively brush the same area. This issue is exaggerated where an incorrect brush is used.

Areas in danger are bony prominences such as elbows and hocks but white or light coloured/ sparse coated breeds will also suffer more than dense coated breeds.

Clipper burns can occur on any dog but those with light coloured coats or sparse coated areas (e.g. Hygiene areas) are more at risk.

22.3.10.2 Prevention

To prevent brush burns, select an appropriate tool. Check that the tool is not too harsh by applying the tool to the back of your hand. Consider the firmness of the bristles and then, if necessary, other options. In the case of dense matted coats, clipping the coat may be a more humane option. If brushing is the best option, section the coat (i.e. select an area to brush), secure the root of the hair by hand (so that brushing will neither cause

Tel: 01283 703043 Email: liza@heavenlyz.com

discomfort nor head movement), then brush in sections from the tip of the hair to the root of the hair. Once all/ most knots and tangles have been removed brush from the root of the hair to the tip of hair.

To prevent clipper burns, ensure that the blade is appropriate to the current part of the grooming process. For example, instead of using a 15mm blade on a white Poodle's coat you, select a 10mm blade that would leave more coat length for additional skin protection. Frequently check the temperature of the blade in use on your wrist and frequently change blades.

22.3.10.3 Signs

- Red moist skin
- Heat
- Swelling
- Pain indicators
- Hair loss

22.3.11 Chemical burn

Read the chemical manufacturers instructions and ensure that they are correctly followed.

If a burn is caused, follow any treatment instructions or call vet for immediate advice. Prevent the dog from self-grooming the affected area by use of a buster or Elizabethan collar.

If the burn is caused by hot fat or grease, gently rub washing up liquid into coat and remove by rinsing in copious amounts of water. Cool skin and coat after removal and then dress the wound in cling film to prevent further damage. Monitor the dog and call vet for advice. Keep the animal under observation always.

22.3.12 Heatstroke

Heatstroke is caused by a pet becoming overheated. Short nosed brachycephalic breeds, obese, elderly, those with underlying health conditions such as heart disease and heavy dense coated dog breeds are most at risk of this condition. The signs of heatstroke are broadly as follows: -

- Panting
- Restless
- Bright red gums
- Incoordination (lack of coordination) and in severe cases collapse
- Unconsciousness.

To treat heatstroke: -

- Cool the entire dog by saturating the coat with tepid water (this aims to reduce core body temperature)
- Phone the Veterinary Surgeon for advice
- Reduce environmental temperature
- Increase ventilation to area
- Do not stop cooling the dog until a veterinary surgeon has arrived
- Do not transport unless advised by the veterinary surgeon

22.3.13 Electrocution

A safe working environment (with electrical items tidied away when not in use) will avoid unnecessary accidents. However, accidents do occur, so to treat electrocution: -

- Isolate the electric source before going near the dog (i.e. turn off the electricity so that, by touching the dog, you do not get electrocuted as well)
- Turn off the power source and move animal away from cable or source with a wooden brush or non-conductible item
- Treat for shock
- Treat any burns

Tel: 01283 703043 Email: liza@heavenlyz.com

- Transport to veterinary surgeon immediately

22.3.14 Fits/ Epilepsy

Usually seen in nervous or over excited dogs between 1 -3 years old. If apparent in older dogs the condition is normally indicated by the owner. This will help you make small adjustments to the salon to reduce the risk of over stressing the dog such as: -

- Continuity, same staff deal with dog throughout the grooming process
- Do not book dogs known to be excessively noisy on the same day as dog's sensitive to fits/ epilepsy
- Schedule dogs susceptible to fits/ epilepsy for last appointment when salon quieter and all other dogs returned to owners.

A fitting dog may collapse on its side and act violently ("convulsions"). Legs are extended, head pulled back and neck extended. Usually, involuntarily chomping of the jaw occurs, with excessive salivation and eyes remaining open with a fixed gaze. The dog may lose control of its bowels and bladder. Most convulsions last for 5-10 minutes. However, the animal may remain in this state for hours, relaxing from one episode and lapsing into another. Seek advice from a veterinary surgeon and contact the dog's owner immediately. Following a fit, the dog may act confused and dazed. Ensure your movements around the dog remain slow to avoid startling. Keep the dog relaxed and calm until the owner arrives. Take the following action: -

- Reduce all environmental stimuli as this will help reduce the attack and the duration of the attack
- Advise owner
- Darken and quieten room
- Remove all obstacles that could injure the animal.
- Pad the room with towels/ bedding to reduce the likelihood of the dog injuring itself when convulsing
- Do not attempt to talk to, or touch, the dog
- Observe quietly and time the fit until owner arrives, instruct owner not to touch or talk to the animal until the fit has passed.

22.3.15 Diabetic Dogs

Plan the groom of these dogs to avoid unnecessary stress and anxiety.

On receipt of a known diabetic dog, ensure that you have discussed a recovery plan in case of problem with the owner.

Observe the dog throughout the grooming process and, if they become ungainly or weak, follow the instructions given by the owner.

Contact the owner.

Drinking water must be available always to the dog.

22.3.16 Accidental Dog Fight

Never attempt to get between two dogs as you are likely to get bitten. The safest way to break up a dogfight requires 2 people to "scruff off" each dog.

To scruff off, grab the dog's scruff (the area at the back of the neck) with both of your hands. Then, with a sharp twist action, forcefully twist the scruff (it needs to be forceful enough to cause pain to the animal). **DO NOT LET GO**. This action will cause the dog pain and encourage it to release whatever it is biting.

If you are not alone, have a colleague to hand to help restrain the dogs. Place the dogs in separate holding units, whilst you attend to the individual dogs' injuries.

If you are on your own, scruff off the dominant dog, then the submissive. Place the dominant dog in a secure holding unit and triage the injuries to the submissive dog first. Once happy that the submissive dog is not in danger, remotely assess the dominant dog – do not put yourself in danger. If you cannot physically attend the dominant dog, seek assistance, potentially from the owner or from your Veterinary surgeon.

22.3.17 Paraphimosis

Paraphimosis is the inability of an engorged penis to retract back into the prepuce following erection or mating. To treat this condition: -

Tel: 01283 703043 Email: liza@heavenlyz.com

- Protect the exposed penis from self-licking as this will damage the sensitive tissue causing further inflammation
- Keep exposed penis wet using water, it is essential that the tissue of the penis does not dry out
- Cold packs may help reduce swelling
- Seek help of veterinary surgeon

22.3.18 Drowning

Drowning occurs when the lungs become flooded with fluid. This prevents the passage of air into the respiratory system and can cause respiratory arrest (i.e. breathing stops).

Excess fluid in the lungs can also cause tissue damage, resulting in reduced ability to absorb oxygen.

Even if an animal does not go into respiratory arrest, damage resulting from fluids in the lungs can result in clinical signs several hours after the incident.

If animal unconscious, treat by ensuring that the tongue is pulled forward (if not, pull it forward). Suspend the animal or raise hind legs to encourage water to leave the chest, squeeze chest or massage gently. Routinely check Airway/ Breathing/ Circulation ("ABC") and resuscitate as needed/ if possible (Heavenlyz offers training in dog resuscitation). Monitor for and manage shock, seek vet advice.

If you suspect that an animal has inhaled water, contact your veterinary practice for advice. The vet may recommend an x-ray to rule out pulmonary oedema (fluid in lung). This is important as secondary drowning can occur several hours later.

22.3.19 Choking/ airway obstruction

Choking/ airway obstruction is a life-threatening emergency.

22.3.19.1 Signs

Lips may be drawn back as dog struggles to breath.

Increased breathing rate or increased effort in trying to breath.

Panic.

Cyanosis - blue or grey mucous membranes.

22.3.19.2 Treatment

The obstruction must be removed. One method is to suspend the animal by its hind legs. This may allow for breathing through the nose as it takes the weight off the larynx and it also helps where the animal is still breathing as they may be able to cough the obstruction out.

If the animal falls unconscious, open mouth, pull tongue to one side and look for presence of foreign body. If found, use appropriate instrument to try and get behind the obstruction and flick it out. Take care not to push the obstruction further into the windpipe.

Consider the use of the Heimlich manoeuvre (Heavenlyz provides practical training): -

- Suspend the dog by the hind legs and apply abdominal thrusts by giving a soft sudden push to the abdomen and towards the diaphragm (In other words, turn the animal upside down, with its back against your chest and hug the animal; place your fists just below the rib-cage - for cats, small dogs and rabbits, use one hand in the same place)
- With both arms, give 5 sharp thrusts (bear hugs) to the abdomen
- Perform each thrust as if it is the one that will expel the object

22.3.20 Shock

When the circulatory system (heart, blood vessels and blood) collapses, shock is the result. Diseases that may produce shock include trauma, heat stroke, heart failure and sepsis.

The clinical signs of shock occur when there is an imbalance of oxygen and nutrients delivered to the cells and the utilisation of oxygen and nutrients.

Shock is a life-threatening response to severe illness or injury that affects many body systems, results in inadequate tissue energy production and can rapidly lead to collapse and death.

Tel: 01283 703043 Email: liza@heavenlyz.com

When there is a disruption of oxygen to the cells, respiration changes from aerobic to anaerobic metabolism. Anaerobic metabolism produces lactic acid which in turn disrupts the acid-base balance of the body.

Types of shock: -

- Hypovolaemic shock occurs when there is severe bleeding or fluid loss and is often associated with trauma, severe dehydration, vomiting or diarrhoea (such as with Parvovirus infection)
- Anaphylactic shock occurs when there is an allergic reaction, such as to an insect sting. Think TV movies!
- Endotoxic shock is caused by the release of toxins from dead Gram-negative
- Septic shock caused by bacteria, such as E. coli, often found in the intestinal tract
- Cardiogenic shock occurs because of heart failure (such as mitral valve disease or cardiomyopathy)

Clinical signs of shock: -

- Rapid weak pulse due to low blood pressure
- Increased heart rate
- Pale mucous membranes and prolonged capillary refill time
- Hypothermia and cold extremities (paws, ears and tail)

Treatment

- Control any bleeding
- If unconscious, place the animal in the 'recovery' position
- Keep patient warm - use blankets/space blankets
- Do not give anything by mouth or use hot water bottles or heating pads
- Seek veterinary care immediately

Tel: 01283 703043 Email: liza@heavenlyz.com

23 Salon Design

23.1 Questions to ask yourself

Before planning your new salon consider the following;

- the salons location (e.g. home salon/ temporary cabin/ permanent building)
- whether you rent or own the premises (and, in the case of the former, whether your lease contract (a) allows the work you want to carry out and (b) supports the term that you have identified in your business plan to at least break even and preferably make profit)
- the budget you must work with, whether the assumptions on which that budget is based will hold and how you will control that budget (e.g. at what stage will payments be made to sub-contractors). When considering budget, remember to discount costs that must be reserved for business rates, insurance, services, etc...
- the expected number of dogs to be groomed daily
- the length of time the dogs will spend with you until collected by owners
- parking
- Health and safety considerations (e.g. even paths/ good lighting)
- Disability access

In the excitement of entering into a whole new venture, students must ensure that they understand any risks and that they exercise appropriate control in making appropriate location, construction, fitting, decoration and equipment choices. The plan for the intended salon work area must be robust and consideration must be made such that the layout supports efficiency and harmony during daily salon operations.

23.2 Choosing the business site

Consider where the premises will be located: -

- Mobile?
- At Home?
- Attached to an existing business? (e.g. kennels, pet shop, veterinary practice)
- Where an existing business already operates?
- Near a competitor?
- Old or new build?
- What catchment will you have? (i.e. will people travel to you)
- A shop or unit

23.3 How you intend to work

The following table sets out a series of advantages and disadvantages for different ways of working within the grooming industry.

Tel: 01283 703043 Email: liza@heavenlyz.com

	Advantages	Disadvantages
As Self-Employed carrying out home visits/ mobile grooming	Fewer overheads Good for nervous dogs No building maintenance	Your security Time wasted getting from one location to another, usually can only do one dog at a time Responsible for insurance and business accounts Vehicle maintenance Isolation? Personal security
As Self-Employed from Home	Low over heads Utilities already installed Can run another business alongside grooming business Child care arrangements easier if work from home	Hard to separate home and work life Can be lonely Responsible for insurance and business accounts Local authority may need to give permission especially for waste disposal and highways traffic control
As Self-Employed in own premises	You're in charge You can dictate own hours and prices You choose how many dogs get groomed You can run other businesses alongside your grooming business Excitement/ challenge/ sense of pride/ sense of achievement More likely to provide other opportunities	High set up cost Higher overheads Long hours Potentially little profit in early years, or even loss Risk of bankruptcy Responsibility for insurance, employees, animals, customers on site, business accounts Change of use permission potentially required from local authority
As Employee	No over heads Your employer caters for tax and N.I. and potentially Pension scheme You get statutory sick pay and holiday entitlement. Employers deals with all running decisions and business concerns	Wages and opportunities can be limited You may have to work at a speed with which you are uncomfortable You may have to work inflexible hours You have less control

Tel: 01283 703043 Email: liza@heavenlyz.com

24 Business Management

24.1 Business Type

Where you intend not to be employed, there are a variety of business models, ranging from sole trader through to franchises. Each option allows for an amount of flexibility in how it is setup and managed and you need to investigate, understand and ultimately decide which better suits your requirements. The following is a general summary of the main types: -

- **SOLE TRADER** – the business is owned and run by you, your liability (in terms of money to be paid out in case of business failure) is unlimited and you may need to supply simple accounts to Her Majesty's Revenue and Customs (HMRC).
- **LIMITED COMPANY** – the business is owned and run by you, your liability (in terms of money to be paid out in case of business failure) is limited by default, you need to supply more complex accounts to HMRC and how you operate is more directly controlled by the companies act. The company is managed on paper by a board of directors (of which you are one).
- **PARTNERSHIP** – the business is owned by one or more persons and can be either sole trader or limited in nature.
- **FRANCHISE** – a franchise is a contractual license to use a business name and trademarks and to sell goods and or services of the franchisor. This business model can allow for a high level of support to you in return for significant (and potentially recurring) payment.

24.2 Business Plan

It is best to formulate a business plan, especially where you expect in the early stages to spend more than you earn or where you intend to look for outside loans or support. A business plan can be as simple or as complex as you wish but, it is important to note that like any plan, realising the appropriate amount of detail will lead to the best outcome. Many government agencies offer business start-up classes and can offer support and advice.

24.3 Financial Management

Financial management is a key attribute to running a business.

If you are running your own business, you will need to ensure that you observe all HMRC regulations.

Even if only for yourself (i.e. where HMRC do not require you to provide accounts, it would be wise to understand money flowing in and out of business).

Financial management requires the keeping of clear and accurate records including the recording of all business income, expenses and all receipts, etc. A Simplex D Accounting book is an easy method of keeping all the records you would be required by law to complete for the Inland Revenue. Alternatively, there are electronic computer/ web based accounts available (e.g. SAGE/ Quickbooks/ etc.).

Sources of advice regards financial management are available. Where you contract the services of an accountant, they will be able to give you advice. Heavenlyz recommend that, for new start-ups at least, weekly book-keeping is a good discipline that will help you understand how well your business is performing. This is especially important if you make changes to how the business operates and, if done weekly (or regularly) will avoid the all too common end of year rush to compile accounts to be submitted to your accountant. Typical Financial Records include the following: -

- supplier's invoices/ receipts
- client invoices/ receipts
- petty cash receipts
- written documentation loans
- card payment terminal receipts and statements
- bank statements, cheque books, paying in books
- chosen payment service method statements (e.g. PayPal®)

Be sure to document every business transaction, file all related papers and work in weeks, months and financial years.

Tel: 01283 703043 Email: liza@heavenlyz.com

24.3.1 Payment methods

Businesses and Clients can agree to exchange payments in several ways. The business should consider all types of payments, including payments in, refunds (partial or whole), credits on account, etc. The following is a selection of payment methods in current use: -

- Cash/ cash equivalents
- Payments in kind ("barter")
- Bankers' Automated Clearing Services (BACS) transfer
- Online payments
- Mobile payments (e.g. Apple or Android pay)
- Vouchers

All the above have a monetary value to the business and will be treated as such by legal/ tax bodies.

24.3.2 Paperwork associated with payment

The following are several items that are associated with payment. They can be issued to clients in paper or electronic form. All the following may include business or personal information and may also include VAT information.

- Invoice – an invoice can either be issued to the client as a request for payment or a record for the client that a payment has been made.
- Receipt – a receipt is normally issued to a client after payment has been made.
- Card payment copies – these are slips of paper printed on card payment specific hardware that are intended to be retained by the cardholder such that they can be reconciled against bank or credit card statements received later
- Credit Note – issued on paper or electronically to indicate that the business owes a specific sum of money to a client. This is normally offset against monies owed by the client.

For a business, it is necessary to keep records of every important transaction for several years, the number stipulated by national tax laws (e.g. by HMRC in the case of the UK). Businesses, when requested, must print receipts for clients and keep copies of client transaction documents.

Clients keep payment documentation for several reasons, including tax purposes and debit/ credit card/ bank statement reconciliation.

In most scenarios covered under this book, the client will not be VAT registered. This is an important note as if the supplier is VAT registered and knows the client to be VAT registered, then the supplier must issue a VAT invoice to the client.

In other cases, issuing an invoice/ receipt by a supplier is significantly determined by any of the following: -

- Request from the client (a receipt must be provided if requested by the client)
- Customer service to the client (i.e. the client may gain customer satisfaction from an unsolicited offer of the receipt)
- Needs of the business (the business process may work better where payment paperwork is issued as standard

In most businesses there will be a designated area for handling payments. Securing this area is obviously important to both the business, its staff and clients. This area can be locked off or kept in plain sight where it can be monitored always. Access to the payment area should be restricted to those who need to deal with payments and there should be a method of auditing any payment actions carried out.

Any software or hardware used to manage payments should be equipped with appropriate virus/ spyware/ malware prevention and the use of firewalls is recommended where there is access to the internet. Any 3rd party equipment used to manage payments must adhere to the law as it applies in the local jurisdiction.

24.3.3 Financial Records and the Law

All paper work or copies of electronic data may be required to be kept for up to 6 years – please check specific regulation on the HMRC website or with your accountant.

Tel: 01283 703043 Email: liza@heavenlyz.com

As soon as you start to set the business up, you may be required to keep a record of all income and expenditure.

HMRC are entitled to inspect financial records of many businesses at any time, so it's essential that you understand your responsibilities in this regard, take time to maintain your records properly and consider seeking appropriate accountancy services verify any accounts.

24.4 Managing accounts

It is important for the business to understand and manage accounts. The key aspects of accounts relating to an animal care business can be explained via the following terms: -

24.4.1 Turnover

Turnover is the total amount billed to clients less any discounts and any VAT

Turnover should be based on the date that goods or services are provided and neither the date of invoice nor the date of payment.

24.4.2 Value Added Tax ("VAT")

VAT varies by jurisdiction but is normally a specific percentage of the value of any product or service provided to clients, where that product or service is subject to VAT.

UK's HMRC body applies different VAT rates based on whether the business needs to be registered for VAT (there are thresholds below which a business does not need to charge VAT), the type of product/ service and the method by which the VAT is calculated/ paid.

The applicable percentage is then added to the charge and submitted to the client. The client pays the "Charge+VAT" price to the business.

The business is required to pay the VAT to HMRC less any VAT spent by the business on VAT allowable expenses. The business must pay this remaining VAT on a regular basis (normally quarterly).

Habitually: -

- the longest time between client paying the VAT portion to the business and the business passing this VAT portion onto HMRC is around 4 months.
- the shortest time between client paying the VAT portion to the business and the business passing this VAT portion onto HMRC is around 1 month.

This means that the VAT received via client payments should largely be retained in the business in preparation to pay the VAT forward to HMRC.

24.4.3 Expenses & "Cost of Goods Sold"

Expenses are monies paid by the business to provide products or services to clients. HMRC define expenses that are and are not allowable.

Allowable expenses will be deducted from turnover to calculate profit, and any business taxes liable on that profit.

Expenses that are not allowable will be on most instances regarded as drawings (personal income) from the business by those who own the business, for which there will be personal taxes liable.

Expenses and "Cost of Goods Sold" (COGS) are largely interchangeable terms. However, in non-trivial businesses, COGS is a valuable measure of how one part of the business is performing when compared to another. For example, if you are providing a dog shampooing service, then the cost of the dog shampoo used for that dog will be both an Expense and a COGS – it will be useful to know this information because if all the COGS involved in the dog shampoo service adds up to an amount that is greater than the charge for the dog shampooing service, then the dog shampooing service is operating at a loss and the business needs to consider any appropriate action.

However, it is more difficult for example to apportion the cost of building repairs to the dog shampooing service. These COGS, and any other potentially hidden COGS, should be carefully considered when reviewing the business, or planning forwards.

24.4.4 Gross Margin

Gross margin is one (of many) business measures of performance. It is a percentage, calculated as follows: -

Tel: 01283 703043 Email: liza@heavenlyz.com

Gross Margin % = (turnover – COGS) / turnover

Gross margin can be applied to the entire business or to individual products or services, or groups of products and services or entire business departments.

Standard gross margin %'s varies per industry and at the time of writing there was no reliable animal care/ dog grooming gross margin % available. However, gross margin can still indicate how the business is performing over time where it is periodically recorded using the same methodology.

The higher the gross margin, the better the business is performing but gross margin remains a comparative calculation.

For example, if 1 year the business's gross margin is 50% and yet the next year it is only 10%, then the business needs to understand why that is and take appropriate action if necessary.

Another example to consider is where you are discussing business performance with another similar business owner. Either both parties will have similar gross margins, or one will be higher than the other. In any case, comparing gross margin alone without reference to the underpinning detail is not a valuable exercise. This is again why it is more important to use gross margin to monitor the performance of your own business over an extended period.

24.4.5 Profit

Profit is essentially turnover less expenses. High, sustainable, profits are highly beneficial. Low profits or losses are obviously to be avoided – the only exception being where a specific area of the business attains low profits but enables high profits (or other benefits) in other areas of the business.

24.4.6 Debtors & Creditors

Debtors are parties that owe money – in the case of a business, these will be parties that owe the business money.

A typical dog grooming business is unlikely to have many debtors or have a significant amount of money owed to the business.

Creditors are parties that are owed money – in the case of a business, these will be parties that are owed money by the business.

Many businesses will owe money to other parties, whether for example that's a premises mortgage, a rent, lease, finance on equipment or products ordered and delivered but yet to be paid.

However, if debt to or credit from the business is significantly increasing or significantly decreasing, then this is indicative of potential business issues. The business should understand why this is occurring before any issues crystallise.

24.5 Taxation

Several sources exist that can provide advice regards business taxation. Any accountancy service will be able to advise you and help maintain relevant records. See Heavenlyz recommended suppliers at the end of this course manual. The following are a selection of the main taxes that may apply to your chosen business model: -

- **Corporation Tax** – A tax on limited companies' taxable income or profits.
- **Value Added Tax (VAT)** – A tax on the final consumption of certain goods and services. Visit the HMRC website for current VAT value and threshold.
- **National Insurance (NI)** – is a contribution from employee earnings to fund various state benefits such as the NHS, State pensions and other welfare related schemes.
- **PAYE** – Pay as you earn is a scheme operated by HM Revenue and Customs to take income tax from employees as they earn it

A key point to remember regards taxation is that in most cases it is still applied retrospectively. This means businesses are required to understand how much tax they owe at any point in time, have enough money in the bank to be able to pay that tax and retain that amount of money until such time that the tax is paid (this can be months later).

24.6 Employing others

Employing others places an obligation on the employer to observe correct employment regulation.

24.6.1 Employment Law

A contract of employment exists as soon as a candidate accepts your job offer. Regardless of any verbal agreement made, a formal contract should be placed in writing within three months of the job offer acceptance.

A written contract of employment terms and conditions must cover specific areas including pay, working hours, entitlement, job title, etc.

Employers must comply with statutory requirements on working hours and leave and the correct National Minimum Wage rate must be met or exceeded.

If a direct employee: -

National Insurance contributions are payable on employees pay and taxable benefits.

Income tax and NI contributions must be deducted at source from their wage and then paid to HM Revenue and customs.

Heavenlyz recommends the use of a payroll service to help maintain employees wage and NI contributions.

Again, see Heavenlyz recommended suppliers at the end of this manual.

24.6.2 Employees Rights

All Employees with more than one-month service are entitled to a notice period and are entitled to be protected from discrimination. Employees must get a pay statement and are entitled to have a discipline and grievance issues dealt with using a fair and reasonable procedure (for the latter, see ACA Code of practice).

Tel: 01283 703043 Email: liza@heavenlyz.com

25 Waste Disposal

You have a legal duty to ensure that all waste generated by the business is disposed of in a safe manner without causing environmental damage. This is called your "Duty of Care". Waste can be broken down into the following types: -

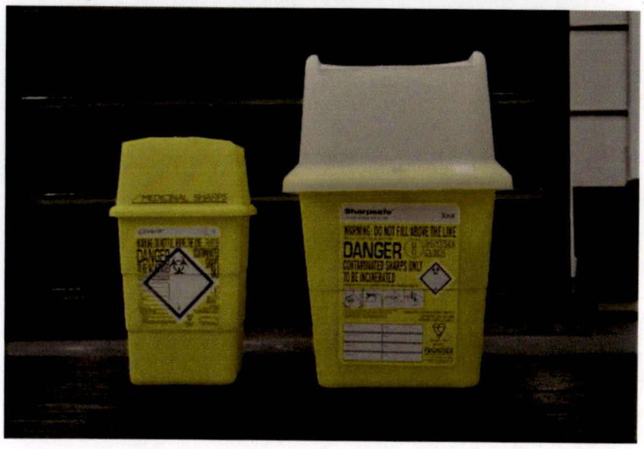

- Clinical Waste
- Household
- Commercial
- These types are summarised in the following sections. It is important to note that in some cases, the waste types are not exclusive. For example, dog faeces can be created via an animal care business, therefore the dog faeces are commercial. However, the dog faeces are also clinical waste.

25.1 Clinical Waste

Clinical waste consists of potential hazardous material, such as the following: -

- Human or animal tissue
- Blood or bodily fluids
- Excretion
- Drugs
- Dressings
- Syringes and needles

Tel: 01283 703043 Email: liza@heavenlyz.com

25.2 Household Waste

Household waste is produced in a domestic manner, may be a mixture of materials originating from a private dwelling.

25.3 Commercial Waste

Commercial waste is solid, non-hazardous, waste generated by a commercial property.

25.4 Organic and Inorganic Waster

There are two types of waste;

- Organic- material which is living or has lived i.e. scraps of food
- Inorganic- Has never lived i.e. plastic

Waste	Type	Disposal Method	PPE
Food	Organic	Special establishment bin, double bag for collection	Gloves, apron
Dog Hair	Organic	Special establishment bin	Gloves, apron, mask
Cleaning Solutions	Inorganic	As per manufacturers recommendation	Gloves, apron, mask
Dog Faeces	Organic	Special establishment's collection. Double bag a doggie bag	Gloves. apron
Records	Organic	Keep up to 6 years. Shred and recycle	Gloves
Electrical Equipment	inorganic	Wrapped and packaged to return to manufacturer or recycle WEEE regulations	Gloves
Glass	Inorganic	Unbroken Place in recyclable glass container or if broken place in wrapped newspaper and dispose in commercial bin	Gloves

Tel: 01283 703043 Email: liza@heavenlyz.com

26Terminology Used in Animal Care/ Grooming

The following is a useful glossary of terms.

Term	Explanation
Anal Glands	Glands which secrete a substance that is used by a dog to mark territory. Located near the anus. Heavenlyz does not recommend that anal glands be expressed, this is a service to be provided by a veterinary surgeon.
Anoestrus	The period of sexual inactivity. On average this lasts 75 days
Apron	Long hair on chest, below the chest bone.
Attachment Comb or snap on	Use of combs on clippers to trim hair to varied lengths (can be used to give a longer/ scissor look).
Bath & Brush	Bathing, including nail trimming, ear cleaning and brush out. Trimming around paws and sanitary areas is included for certain breeds, such as Golden retrievers, Shelties, Collies, and Huskies.
Beard	Long hair on muzzle
Bitch	Female dog
Blaster/ High velocity dryer	Dryer used to remove excess water and dead coat from dogs, aids drying process. Conditioner can also be blasted into the wet coat of a dog during the bathing process, to help aid in the coat conditioning of damaged dry hair.
Blaze	White stripe running down centre of face
Brachycephalic	A descriptive term for animals whose skulls or noses are shorter than typical for the species
Brachygnathism	This is an undershot bite, occurring when the lower jaw protrudes beyond the upper jaw. Though strictly a bred abnormality, this is considered normal for brachycephalic breeds, such as Bulldogs and Pugs
Breed Standard	The set of breed descriptions originally laid down by various breed clubs and accepted officially by international bodies.
Brick Shaped Head	Skull and muzzle the same width (e.g. fox terrier)
Cabinet dryer	Dryer which produces warm air were dogs can either sit or stand to dry.
Canker	Serious infection noted for the fowl, pungent odour and dark-coloured discharge. Habitually found in a dog's ear.
Carding	A natural technique to remove the loose coat from many coat types. One of the most popular techniques used in the salon today. The carding technique helps to maintain a healthy coat by removing the undercoat and helps to prevent shedding. It can be used on silky coats, wire coated terriers, schnauzers and on smooth coats to remove loose coat.
Castrate	To remove testicles
Cat Feet	Round compact cushioned feet

Tel: 01283 703043 Email: liza@heavenlyz.com

Term	Explanation
Chalking	Chalking the coat is a procedure used before hand-stripping to allow for a better grip on the hair. Chalking is also used to whiten the coat on areas that are stained such as around the eyes, feet, anal and hock areas.
Chondrodysplastic	Pertaining to a defect in development of cartilage, especially of long bones, resulting in arrested growth and dwarfism
Clipper Burn	General term used to describe two conditions: - 1. Use of a blade that is cutting coat too short causing irritation to the skin (can be a side effect of stripping a severely matted coat even if correct blade size is used!) 2. Heating of a blade by friction that causes a superficial burn. (check your blade is not running too hot, remember to frequently change blades or use appropriate lubrication as necessary)
Clipping	A technical skill that is used on many breeds, using electric clippers with different blade lengths to reduce the length of a dog's coat.
Coat King	Tool used for removing dead undercoat and for giving a natural hand-stripped look. Comes in different sizes from fine to coarse. Can be used on silky coated gundogs and wire coats.
Cryptorchid	When one or both testicles fail to descend into the scrotum
Ctenocephalides	Dog or Cat Flea
Cystitis	Inflammation of the bladder, usually caused by a bladder infection
Dam	Mother dog
De-matting comb	Will help split through knots and tangles. Can be used on long haired coat types.
De-matting rake	Will help split through knots and tangles and impacted undercoat.
Dermatitis	Any inflammation of the skin; used to describe several different skin rashes that are either caused by infections, allergies or irritating substances; advise the owner to seek the advice of a veterinary surgeon and make a note of that advice on the record card you keep for the dog
Dew Claws	Claws found slightly higher up the inside hind and fore legs, can be single or double clawed.
Digit	Toe
Dioestrus or Met-oestrus	Stage when bitch is unmated, during this stage a bitch may show signs of a false pregnancy. On average, this lasts 90 days
Dipylidium Caninum	Common tape worm
Docked Tail	Tail that has been amputated to a certain length. This is only necessary for medical reasons – Heavenlyz does not support the docking of tails for cosmetic purposes.
Dolichocephalic	A condition where the head is longer than would be expected, relative to its width

Tel: 01283 703043 Email: liza@heavenlyz.com

Term	Explanation
Dry Drowning	A small amount of water enters the lungs forming fluid accumulation in the lung's air spaces ("pulmonary oedema"). This can happen several hours after ingress of water and can be fatal.
Ear Types	There can be a vast variation of ear shape, but generally there are 3 categories that apply: - 1. Erect or Pricked ear, e.g. West Highland white terrier 2. Drop or Pendant Ear, e.g. Spaniel 3. Semi-dropped, e.g. Fox Terrier or Collie Heavenlyz does not support the surgical pricking of ears for cosmetic purposes.
Ear Cleaning	Use of cleaner and cotton balls to remove dirt, oils, and build up in the outer opening of ear; certain breeds such as Poodles and Schnauzers also require the hair in the ear canal to be removed by being plucked. Caution; never put any instrument or powder down a dog's ear canal, the use of correct technique of finger and thumb and aid of ear powder is all that is necessary to remove ear hair safely. It is controversial to pluck any hair that is not easily removed with finger and thumb. The dog should not feel pain and the ear should not be left reddened or sore. This goes against the five animal needs.
Ear Infection	Can be caused by bacteria and/ or fungus. Signs of an ear infection include pungent odour discharge, redness, swelling and pain on examination; advise owners to seek veterinary attention and make a note on client card with advice you have given.
Easy epilation	Easy epilation refers to the ability to easily remove excessive quantities of hair with little resistance
Ectoparasites	External parasites
Ectropion	A medical condition in which the lower eyelid turns outwards
Endoparasites	Internal Parasites
Entropion	A medical condition in which the eyelid (usually the lower lid) folds inward
Epistaxis	Refers to bleeding from the nose
Fall	Hair overhanging the face
Feathering	Longer hair flowing from legs, skirt, ears, body and tail
Feathers/ Furnishing	Longer hair on the legs, under body, tail.
Felt	A patch of felt-like to the touch, densely compacted, under-coat or top-coat hairs
Felting	Occurs when the undercoat attempts to shed, is trapped by a poorly maintained top coat and is then held together with that topcoat in a Felt
Flea comb	Very fine-toothed comb ideal for checking for Ectoparasites (e.g. fleas).
FURminator®	Specialized de-shedding tool. Helps remove hair from smooth and double coated breeds (e.g. German shepherds). Can also be used on cats and rabbits.

Tel: 01283 703043 Email: liza@heavenlyz.com

Term	Explanation
Gait	Movement of dogs when walking or standing
Gingivitis	Inflammation of the gum tissue
Groom	Everything with the bath & brush, but with the inclusion of hair styling/ trim specific to the pet's breed.
Grooming Scissors - Curved scissors:	Used for shaping coats.
Grooming Scissors - Straight	Used for general trimming.
Grooming Scissors - Thinning scissors	Used for blending and thinning out coats. Available single sided (where one side has a straight blade) and double-sided.
Hand-stripping	Hand-stripping is a labour-intensive method of removing wire/ silky coat. It helps retain the proper coat texture and colour required for specific breeds/ coat types. The alternative to hand-stripping is removing the coat by clipping, scissoring or thinning, rather than pulling the dead hair from the hair follicle. Hand-stripping is mostly used on show dogs. However, pets with the correct texture of coat can be hand stripped in a modified way that will still retain colour and texture of the coat, without taking hours.
Heat	Dog in season
High velocity/ blaster drying	A rapid airflow drying tool - the most efficient drying tool in a typical salon. The dryer is adaptable to a variety of coat types and has numerous uses, including de-shedding and loosening matted coats. High velocity drying is a technique that can be used as the second step to remove excessive moisture from the coat after the first step of towel drying. It helps to straighten the coat in wool coated breeds prior to heat dying and can help prevent brush burn, heat stress and repetitive strain injury to the groomer by saving time brushing and the reduced amount of heat to the dog.
Hound Glove	These come in a range of textures of plastic or rubber or with short bristles or wire. Used on short haired dogs to gently remove dead hair or finish polishing the coat.
Hygiene clip	Performing a trim around the sanitary areas, belly, and armpits.
Impaction	A condition where the secretions in the anal glands harden, causing swelling, inflammation, and pain; if left untreated, can cause infection and/or abscess; must be treated by vet immediately.
Ixodes Canisuga	Tick
Kennel Drying/ Cage Drying	Kennel or cage drying is a method of drying the dog's coat while the pet is in a kennel. The bather places the dog in a thermostatically controlled kennel equipped with vents and blowers (but ensures monitoring of the dog always).

Tel: 01283 703043 Email: liza@heavenlyz.com

Term	Explanation
Matt	A matt is a mixture of coat that has tangled due to lack of brushing. Some mats which are not close to the skin can be split/ brushed out. In cases were the matting is felted tight to the skin it would be inhumane to try and brush these out. The only alternative may be to completely shave the coat with a short blade. This will remove the matt without the pain of tugging on the skin. Caution: Heat burns may be caused by close clipping, monitor your blade temperature, replace or cool lube regularly.
Matt Breaker	Will help break through matts and tangles.
Matt splitter	Cuts through mats must be used with great care.
Mesocephalic	Having a head that is not particularly short or long from front to back (relative to its width from left to right)
Monorchid	Having one testicle that has not descended into the scrotum
Moulting	Shedding of the coat usually seasonal
Nail Quick	Blood vessels in the nails. Infrequent trimming can cause quick to elongate, causing the nails to be excessively long even after trimming.
Oestrus	This is the stage where the bitch will accept mating. The vulva is much enlarged, the discharge is straw colour rather than blood stained, ovulation usually is spontaneous within 2 days of start of oestrus. On average, this lasts 9 days
Otodectes	Ear mite
Paraphimosis	Paraphimosis is the inability to retract the erect penis back within the prepuce. This usually occurs in dogs following sexual stimulation.
Phantom Pregnancy	Having the appearance of clinical or subclinical signs and symptoms associated with pregnancy when not actually pregnant
Pin Brush	Ideal for dogs with sensitive skin and show coats and long silky coats as it will not break the hair.
Poodle Face/ Feet/ Tail	Also known as clean face/ feet/ tail; Feet & face & tail shaved with a 15/ 10 blade; Applies to Poodles only
PPE	Personal Protective Equipment
Prognathism	Overshot bite occurs when the upper jaw protrudes beyond the lower jaw. This is abnormal for any breed
Pro-oestrus	The beginning of the bitch's heat. Vulva is swollen, there is blood staining, although bitch attracts attention of male dog she will not allow them to mate her. On average this lasts 9 days
Rosette	A swirl of hair growing in a different direction to main coat
Rough Clip	Clipping the excess hair of the coat prior to bathing. Can be used to remove matted coat or excess heavy coat to aid/ reduce drying and brushing out time.
Scissoring	Use of scissors to trim and sculpt the pet's hair

Tel: 01283 703043 Email: liza@heavenlyz.com

Term	Explanation
Shedding blade:	Used to loosen dead hair on smooth and double coated
Slicker Brush:	A handled flat brush with pins (in either soft, medium or hard) used to remove matts and tangles from all coats except silk coats. Caution; Groomers must be careful to brush from the skin outwards and not grate or graze the skin leading to brush burn from over brushing in one spot. Caution regards sensitive or bony areas e.g. elbows, knuckles on feet, never brush over penis/ vulva, avoid eyes and nose etc.
Spayed bitch ("bitch spay")	Neutered female dog
Spondylosis	Spondylosis Deformans is a condition that affects the vertebral bones of the spine and is characterized by the presence of bony spurs or ***'osteophytes'*** along the edges of the bones of the spine. A bony spur may develop in a single spot on the spine; more commonly, there will be multiple bone spurs. The most common places that spondylosis deformans lesions develop are along the thoracic vertebrae (chest), especially at the junction between the rib cage and the abdomen, in the lumbar spine (lower back) and in the lumbosacral spine (around the hips and back legs). Spondylosis deformans is a chronic condition that is associated with ageing.
Stand dryer	Heat dryer used to dry dogs.
Strip	To shave the pet down to the skin all over; only suggested where removing severe matting.
Stripping Knife	Used for hand-stripping comes in a variety of sizes. Used for removing clipper marks, taking out excess undercoat and finishing of hand-stripped breeds.
Toxascaris Leonina & Toxocara Cani	Common round worms
Undercoat	Shorter hair found under the top coat
Undercoat rakes	These come in long and short pinned versions for removing. Undercoat from double coated breeds.
Utility Cut/ Clip off	A hair cut that is more for the convenience of the owner and pet than for the correct styling of pet; can also be done due to poor coat condition, age, behaviour, environmental conditions and health of pet.

Tel: 01283 703043 Email: liza@heavenlyz.com

27 Thank you!

27.1 Acknowledgements

Heavenlyz would like to acknowledge all contributors of photographs to this manual and would especially like to thank: -

- Furst Class Lounge, Foxwood Close, Foxwood Park, Chesterfield, Derbyshire, S41 9RB, Tel: 01246 453545 (http://www.furstclasslounge.co.uk)
- Allbreed Grooming Academy, 11 High Oak Brierley Hill, West Midlands DY5 4LA, Tel: 01384 483617 (http://www.allbreedgrooming.com)
- The Pet Studio, The Grange/Smallway, Bristol BS49 5AA

27.2 Other Heavenlyz Services

In addition to consultancy services in animal care and related businesses Heavenlyz can provide the following additional services: -

- Education, examination and fast-track routes to qualifications
- Salon Set up & Management Consultations
- Assessments in your workplace
- Training via our accredited satellite centres

Contact us for further information on 01283 703043 or liza@heavenlyz.com.

27.3 Further education

Other Heavenlyz courses are available and are highly recommended.

- Theory Revision Workshop
- City & Guilds Level 2 & Level 3 Diploma in Dog Grooming
- OCN Level 3 Diploma in Dog Grooming
- Level 3 Pet First Aid Certification
- OCN Level 3 Cat Grooming Certificate
- Diploma Workshop and examination
- Teaching and Assessment Qualifications
- Dog Walking
- Pet Sitting

27.4 Further orders

This manual is updated from time to time. If you would like additional copies, then please contact us.

27.5 Contact us

If you need to, you can contact the Heavenlyz team via: -

Telephone:	01283 703043	Facebook:	www.facebook.com/Heavenlyz
Email:	Liza@heavenlyz.com	Twitter:	www.twitter.com/HeavenlyzUKNI

27.6 Heavenlyz Recommended Suppliers

Heavenlyz have used the following suppliers of products and services from time to time in the past. They may be of equal use to you, especially if you are setting up or running your own business. If you do contact them, please mention that Heavenlyz referred you: -

- Accountancy – Bernard Rogers & Co, Bank Gallery, High Street, Kenilworth, Warwickshire, CV8 1LY. Tel 01926 851516. Web www.bernard-rogers.co.uk
- Insurance – Adrian Strangwick of HIA international, Tel: 01234 346495. Web http://hiaint.com/

27.7 Further Reading

Heavenlyz recommends the following reference books: -

- "Canine Terminology" by Harold R. Spira, ISBN 9780949284297
- "Grooming Manual for the Dog and Cat" ISBN 9781405111836
- "Notes from the Grooming Table" ISBN 9780975412800
- "The Allbreed Dog Grooming Guide" by Sam Kohl ISBN 9780964607248
- "The Kennel Club Illustrated Breed Standards" ISBN 9780091928544
- "Theory of 5" ISBN 9780975412862